GREAT GRAPH ART
Decimals & Fractions

By Cindi Mitchell

SCHOLASTIC
PROFESSIONAL BOOKS

NEW YORK • TORONTO • LONDON • AUCKLAND • SYDNEY
MEXICO CITY • NEW DELHI • HONG KONG

To my sister Christi Offutt,
who is living proof that a pesky younger sister
can turn into a wonderful, trusted friend.

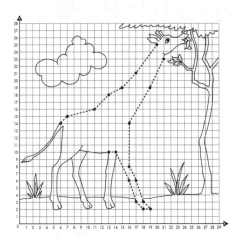

Cover design by Norma Ortiz
Interior design by Solutions by Design, Inc.
Interior illustrations by Kate Flanagan

ISBN 0-590-64375-4

Contents

When I taught fifth and sixth grade, my students couldn't wait to begin our math unit on coordinate graphing. I was amazed as I watched them spend hours laboring over plotting points and connecting them with straight lines. They were eager to see an image emerge and would often take guesses about what it was going to be. Long after our graphing unit was over, my students begged for graphing activities. They never seemed to tire of them, and when my supply ran out, they started making their own.

Like most teachers, I was always on the lookout for fun activities that would encourage my students to practice basic math skills. I decided to pair kids' love of graphing with skills practice. It was a winning combination. This book is a compilation of those activities. Here's how they work.

How to Use This Book

Each activity consists of two pages—a graph page and a worksheet of math problems. First, students read a riddle at the top of the graph page. For example, the riddle for Speedy Traveler (pages 11–12) poses the question *What travels at a high rate of speed and is spelled the same forward and backward?* Students then look at the corresponding page of instructions and solve decimal or fraction problems to find ordered number pairs. They then plot the ordered pairs on the graph and connect the points with a straightedge to complete a

picture, which is the solution to the riddle. In this activity, students plot and connect points to make a race car. Something that travels at a high rate of speed and is spelled the same forward and backward is a race car!

Allow two days to complete each activity. On the first day, have students solve decimal or fraction problems and check their answers to make sure they are correct. The following day, let them plot the points, create the picture, and solve the riddle!

How to Begin

Choose one or two activities to introduce and teach coordinate graphing. Then use the others to reinforce your study of decimals and fractions, or use the activities to teach a unit on graphing. The skill focus of each activity appears at the top of each activity page. You'll also find the math skills listed in the Contents on page 3.

After students have finished graphing the pictures, have them add their personal creative touch by coloring them with crayons or colored pencils. Then display the picture graphs in a prominent place in your classroom.

Taking It Further

Let students create their own graph art designs using the reproducibles on pages 61 and 62.

On page 61, encourage them to draw a simple design that has no more than nine or ten points. Beside each point, have them write the ordered pair that identifies it in parentheses.

On the worksheet on page 62, tell students to write the ordered pairs in the order they should be connected. Remind them to write the word "STOP" if they want to end a line after a particular ordered pair.

Now the fun begins. Give each student a blank copy of the graph on page 61. Then let students swap their completed worksheet pages with a classmate and try to recreate each other's original designs. Have fun!

Cindi Mitchell

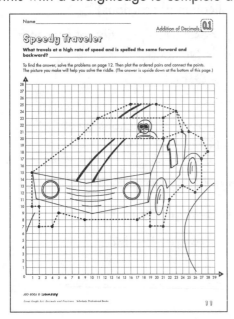

Name_____

Baseball and Birthdays

What do baseball teams and birthday cakes have in common? _____

To find the answer, solve the problems on page 6. Then plot the ordered pairs and connect the points.
The picture you make will help you solve the riddle. (The answer is upside down at the bottom of this page.)

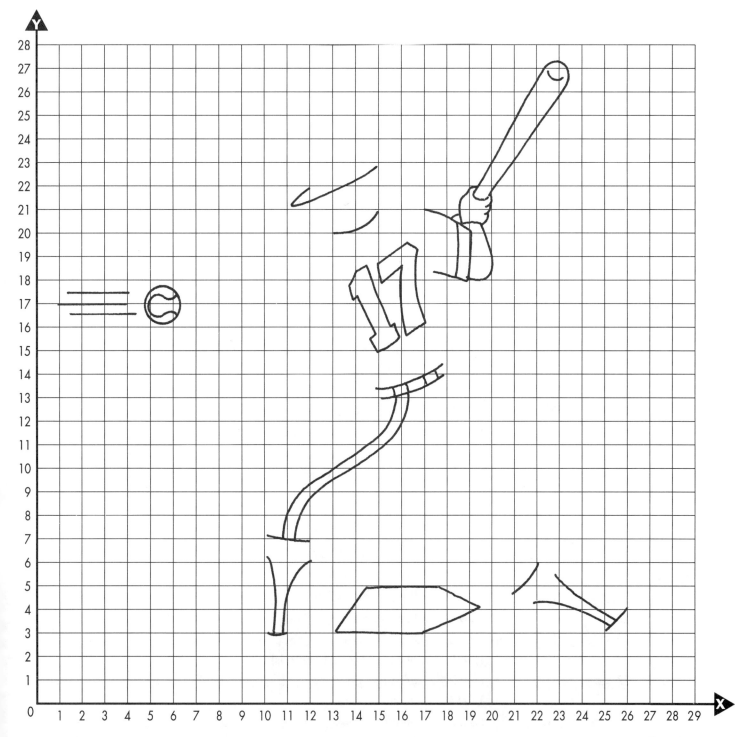

Answer: They both have batters.

Baseball and Birthdays

1 Look at number 1, below. The number in the first column is the X coordinate in an ordered pair.

2 Look at the second column. Circle the number in the ones, tens, hundreds, thousands, tenths, hundredths, or thousandths place (or a combination of any two), as indicated in parentheses. The number you circle is the Y coordinate.

3 Write the X and Y coordinates in the third column to make an ordered pair. The first one has been done for you.

4 Determine the ordered pairs for the rest of the chart.

5 Plot the ordered pairs on the graph on page 5 in the order they are given. Then use a straightedge to connect the points in the order you plotted them. Can you solve the riddle?

	X Coordinate	Y Coordinate		Ordered Pair
1.	8	34.1	(tenths)	(8, 1)
2.	9	59.021	(thousandths)	
3.	11	2.321	(hundredths)	
4.	11	217.3	(tenths)	
5.	12	15.41	(ones)	
6.	12	4.179	(hundredths)	
7.	17	9,107.9	(hundred and tens)	
8.	20	55.002	(tens)	
9.	25	8.563	(thousandths)	
10.	24	5.712	(hundredths)	
11.	25	15.2	(tens)	
12.	27	9,400.5	(hundreds)	
13.	26	0.94	(hundredths)	
14.	22	6,024	(thousands)	
15.	20	8.102	(tenths and hundredths)	
16.	20	6.912	(hundredths and thousandths)	
17.	18	8.148	(tenths and hundredths)	
18.	17	21.9	(tens and ones)	
19.	15	2,194.2	(thousands and hundreds)	
20.	15	0.823	(hundredths and thousandths)	
21.	14	244	(hundreds and tens)	
22.	13	24.18	(tens and ones)	
23.	12	6.022	(hundredths and thousandths)	
24.	13	1.20	(tenths and hundredths)	
25.	11	9.19	(tenths and hundredths)	
26.	13	1,744	(thousands and hundreds)	
27.	15	13.98	(tens and ones)	
28.	10	0.91	(tenths)	
29.	10	4.223	(thousandths)	
30.	8	41.2	(ones)	

Great Graph Art: Decimals and Fractions Scholastic Professional Books

Name_____

The Breakfast of Scarecrows

What does a scarecrow eat for breakfast? _____

To find the answer, solve the problems on page 8. Then plot the ordered pairs and connect the points. The picture you make will help you solve the riddle. (The answer is upside down at the bottom of this page.)

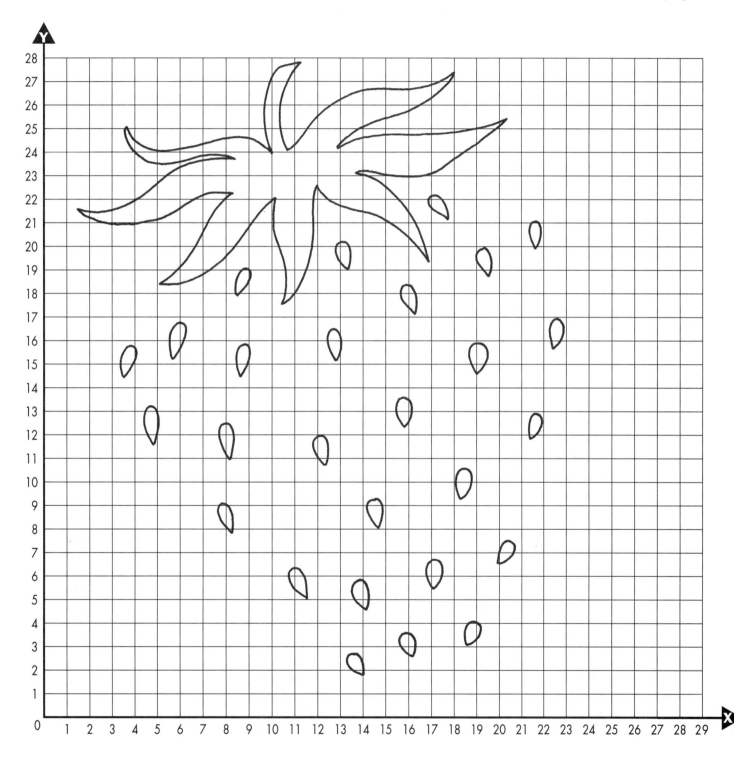

Answer: strawberries

Name_____

The Breakfast of Scarecrows

1 Look at number 1, below. The number in the first column is the X coordinate in an ordered pair.

2 Look at the numbers in the second column. Use < or > to compare the two numbers. The number(s) in the tenth (or hundredth place if there is one) of the larger number is the Y coordinate.

3 Write the X and Y coordinates in the third column to make an ordered pair. The first one has been done for you.

4 Determine the ordered pairs for the rest of the chart.

5 Plot the ordered pairs on the graph on page 7 in the order they are given. Then use a straightedge to connect the points in the order you plotted them. Can you solve the riddle?

	X Coordinate	Y Coordinate		Ordered Pair
1.	5	5.21 > 5.09		(5, 21)
2.	2	15.09 ____ 15.15		
3.	2	9.12 ____ 8.9		
4.	4	0.8 ____ 0.09		
5.	14	3.02 ____ 4.0		
6.	16	19.10 ____ 20.0		
7.	17	7.1 ____ 7.01		
8.	19	12.02 ____ 12.1		
9.	21	0.4 ____ 0.098		
10.	25	7.14 ____ 7.111		
11.	25	2.09 ____ 2.16		
12.	24	22.19 ____ 21.48		
13.	23	2.21 ____ 1.22		
14.	19	0.023 ____ 0.23		
15.	17	7.23 ____ 7.203		

Great Graph Art: Decimals and Fractions   Scholastic Professional Books

Name_____

High Flier

Why did the pilot flunk out of school? _____

To find the answer, solve the problems on page 10. Then plot the ordered pairs and connect the points.
The picture you make will help you solve the riddle. (The answer is upside down at the bottom of this page.)

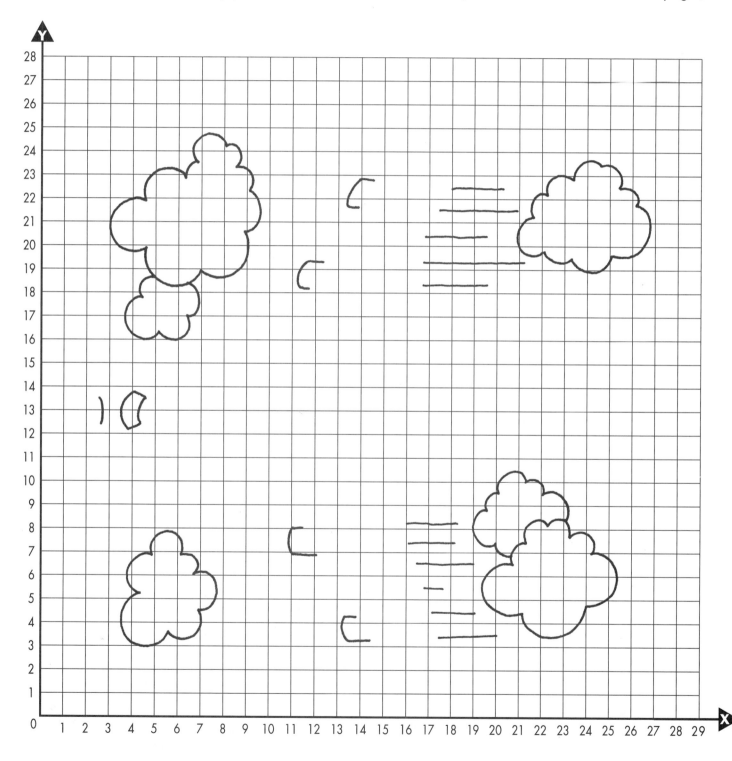

Answer: He had his head in the clouds.

Name_____

High Flier

1. Look at number 1, below. The number in the first column is the X coordinate in an ordered pair.

2. Look at the number in the second column. Round it to the nearest whole number. The new number is the Y coordinate.

3. Write the X and Y coordinates in the third column to make an ordered pair. The first one has been done for you.

4. Determine the ordered pairs for the rest of the chart.

5. Plot the ordered pairs on the graph on page 7 in the order they are given. Then use a straightedge to connect the points in the order you plotted them. Can you solve the riddle?

	X Coordinate	Y Coordinate	Ordered Pair
1.	18	0.512 = __1__	(18, 1)
2.	15	8.3 = _____	
3.	15	11.87 = _____	
4.	23	12.491 = _____	
5.	25	12.59 = _____	
6.	27	9.003 = _____	
7.	28	8.901 = _____	
8.	27	13.067 = _____	
9.	28	16.7 = _____	
10.	27	17.2 = _____	
11.	25	13.47 = _____	
12.	23	13.99 = _____	
13.	15	14.47 = _____	
14.	15	18.06 = _____	
15.	18	25.39 = _____	
16.	16	24.90 = _____	
17.	9	13.9 = _____	
18.	3	13.756 = _____	
19.	2	13.117 = _____	
20.	3	11.5 = _____	
21.	9	12.112 = _____	
22.	16	1.24 = _____	
23.	18	0.84 = _____	

Great Graph Art: Decimals and Fractions Scholastic Professional Books

Name_____

Speedy Traveler

What travels at a high rate of speed and is spelled the same forward and backward? _____

To find the answer, solve the problems on page 12. Then plot the ordered pairs and connect the points. The picture you make will help you solve the riddle. (The answer is upside down at the bottom of this page.)

Answer: a race car

Speedy Traveler

1. Look at number 1, below. The number in the first column is the X coordinate in an ordered pair.

2. On a separate sheet of paper, solve the problem in the second column. Write your answer on the blank line. The whole number in your answer is the Y coordinate.

3. Write the X and Y coordinates in the third column to make an ordered pair. The first one has been done for you.

4. Determine the ordered pairs for the rest of the chart.

5. Plot the ordered pairs on the graph on page 11 in the order they are given. Then use a straightedge to connect the points in the order you plotted them. After you come to the word "STOP," start a new line. Can you solve the riddle?

	X Coordinate	Y Coordinate	Ordered Pair
1.	21	17.34 + 5.81 = __23.15 = 23__	(21, 23)
2.	23	8.09 + 15.99 = _____	
3.	24	7.142 + 13.916 = _____	
4.	21	4.1 + 16.23 = _____	
5.	21	11.354 + 12.19 = _____	
6.	11	3.95 + 19.7 = _____	
7.	8	19.07 + 1.91 = _____	
8.	21	7.45 + 13.05 = _____	STOP
9.	11	11.49 + 11.51 = _____	
10.	16	17.46 + 7.57 = _____	
11.	20	9.72 + 15.37 = _____	
12.	23	7.098 + 16.909 = _____	
13.	25	9 + 12.9 = _____	
14.	27	8.73 + 11.5 = _____	
15.	27	14.73 + 3.78 = _____	
16.	28	6.9 + 10.8 = _____	
17.	27	5.12 + 8.81 = _____	
18.	26	0.481 + 11.6 = _____	
19.	24	7.425 + 6.013 = _____	
20.	22	6.37 + 4.69 = _____	
21.	21	2.85 + 4.89 = _____	
22.	19	4.9 + 2.1 = _____	
23.	19	7.77 + 1.831 = _____	
24.	17	2.21 + 6.6 = _____	
25.	9	5.5 + 2.6 = _____	
26.	5	7.8 + 1.93 = _____	
27.	4	6.21 + 1.021 = _____	
28.	2	1.8 + 5.31 = _____	
29.	2	2.003 + 8.7 = _____	
30.	1	9.21 + 1.021 = _____	
31.	1	7.8 + 7.31 = _____	
32.	8	15.003 + 5.7 = _____	

Great Graph Art: Decimals and Fractions Scholastic Professional Books

Name_____

Heart Attack

What is the number one cause of a heart attack? _____

To find the answer, solve the problems on page 14. Then plot the ordered pairs and connect the points. The picture you make will help you solve the riddle. (The answer is upside down at the bottom of this page.)

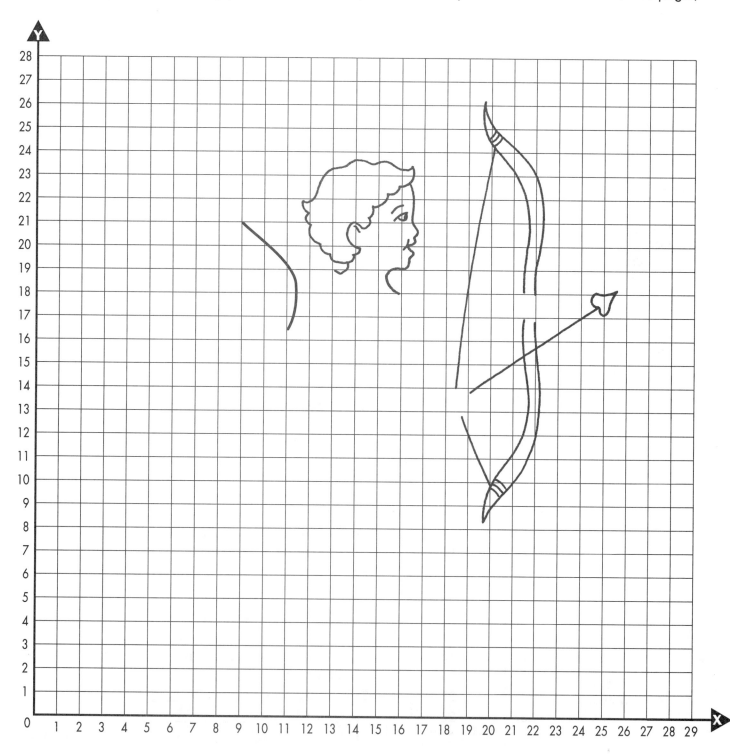

Answer: Cupid

Heart Attack

1. Look at number 1, below. The number in the first column is the X coordinate in an ordered pair.

2. On a separate sheet of paper, solve the problem in the second column. Write your answer on the blank line. The dollar amount in your answer is the Y coordinate.

3. Write the X and Y coordinates in the third column to make an ordered pair. The first one has been done for you.

4. Determine the ordered pairs for the rest of the chart.

5. Plot the ordered pairs on the graph on page 13 in the order they are given. Then use a straight-edge to connect the points in the order you plotted them. Can you solve the riddle?

	X Coordinate	Y Coordinate	Ordered Pair
1.	13	$12.14 + $6.89 = $19.03 = $19	(13, 19)
2.	10	$18.09 + $4.08 = _____	
3.	9	$15.11 + $5.90 = _____	
4.	8	$13.99 + $8.75 = _____	
5.	1	$3.64 + $8.79 = _____	
6.	5	$5.55 + $8.80 = _____	
7.	6	$4.05 + $8.00 = _____	
8.	9	$11.07 + $4.91 = _____	
9.	10	$4.45 + $9.05 = _____	
10.	11	$8.07 + $7.20 = _____	
11.	11	$10.49 + $2.51 = _____	
12.	10	$5.36 + $6.05 = _____	
13.	9	$5.72 + $0.45 = _____	
14.	6	$2.99 + $0.99 = _____	
15.	7	$0.75 + $0.90 = _____	
16.	7	$1.85 + $1.15 = _____	
17.	11	$4.90 + $0.88 = _____	
18.	13	$2.19 + $6.01 = _____	
19.	17	$5.94 + $2.17 = _____	
20.	18	$1.42 + $2.73 = _____	
21.	21	$3.44 + $0.99 = _____	
22.	19	$2.95 + $2.99 = _____	
23.	19	$8.30 + $2.10 = _____	
24.	17	$4.89 + $6.76 = _____	
25.	15	$1.14 + $10.60 = _____	
26.	15	$0.57 + $14.19 = _____	
27.	19	$2.39 + $10.89 = _____	
28.	19	$9.01 + $5.21 = _____	
29.	18	$9.87 + $4.39 = _____	
30.	16	$7.33 + $8.77 = _____	
31.	21	$15.11 + $2.12 = _____	
32.	22	$8.93 + $8.79 = _____	
33.	22	$12.49 + $5.55 = _____	
34.	16	$9.09 + $9.45 = _____	

Great Graph Art: Decimals and Fractions Scholastic Professional Books

Homework Helper

What kind of insect can best help you with your spelling homework? _____

To find the answer, solve the problems on page 16. Then plot the ordered pairs and connect the points. The picture you make will help you solve the riddle. (The answer is upside down at the bottom of this page.)

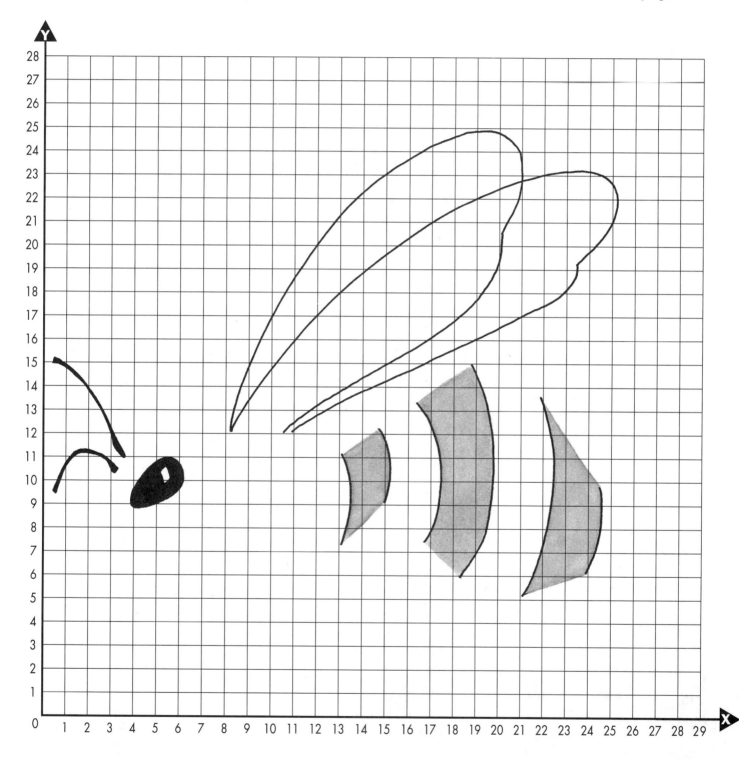

Name_____

Homework Helper

1 Look at number 1, below. The number in the first column is the X coordinate in an ordered pair.

2 On a separate sheet of paper, solve the problem in the second column. Write your answer on the blank line. The whole number in your answer is the Y coordinate.

3 Write the X and Y coordinates in the third column to make an ordered pair. The first one has been done for you.

4 Determine the ordered pairs for the rest of the chart.

5 Plot the ordered pairs on the graph on page 15 in the order they are given. Then use a straightedge to connect the points in the order you plotted them. Each time you come to the word "STOP," start a new line. Can you solve the riddle?

	X Coordinate	Y Coordinate	Ordered Pair
1.	7	$19.74 - 8.39 =$ __11.35 = 11__	(7, 11)
2.	6	$16.59 - 4.42 =$ _____	
3.	4	$31.09 - 18.7 =$ _____	
4.	2	$9.9 - 1.77 =$ _____	
5.	3	$14.7 - 6.31 =$ _____	
6.	1	$8 - 1.01 =$ _____	
7.	6	$13.95 - 5.45 =$ _____	
8.	7	$28.07 - 20.27 =$ _____	
9.	13	$19.45 - 12.3 =$ _____	
10.	15	$32.45 - 23.3 =$ _____	
11.	19	$17 - 11.51 =$ _____	
12.	21	$31.19 - 25.29 =$ _____	
13.	24	$39.76 - 33.33 =$ _____	
14.	25	$7.7 - 4.69 =$ _____	
15.	25	$13.098 - 3.971 =$ _____	
16.	21	$25.9 - 10.3 =$ _____	
17.	19	$36.393 - 20.703 =$ _____	
18.	13	$16.129 - 4.859 =$ _____	
19.	11	$43.12 - 31.09 =$ _____	
20.	8	$17.4 - 4.92 =$ _____	
21.	7	$25.19 - 14.19 =$ _____	STOP
22.	10	$18.16 - 9.15 =$ _____	
23.	9	$12.05 - 3.9 =$ _____	
24.	11	$16.9 - 12.3 =$ _____	
25.	10	$15.704 - 11.703 =$ _____	STOP
26.	12	$13.98 - 4.7 =$ _____	
27.	11	$39.13 - 31 =$ _____	
28.	13	$8.36 - 4.18 =$ _____	
29.	12	$13.3 - 9.3 =$ _____	

Great Graph Art: Decimals and Fractions Scholastic Professional Books

Mouse Trap

What is the name of the world's fastest mouse trap?_____

To find the answer, solve the problems on page 18. Then plot the ordered pairs and connect the points. The picture you make will help you solve the riddle. (The answer is upside down at the bottom of this page.)

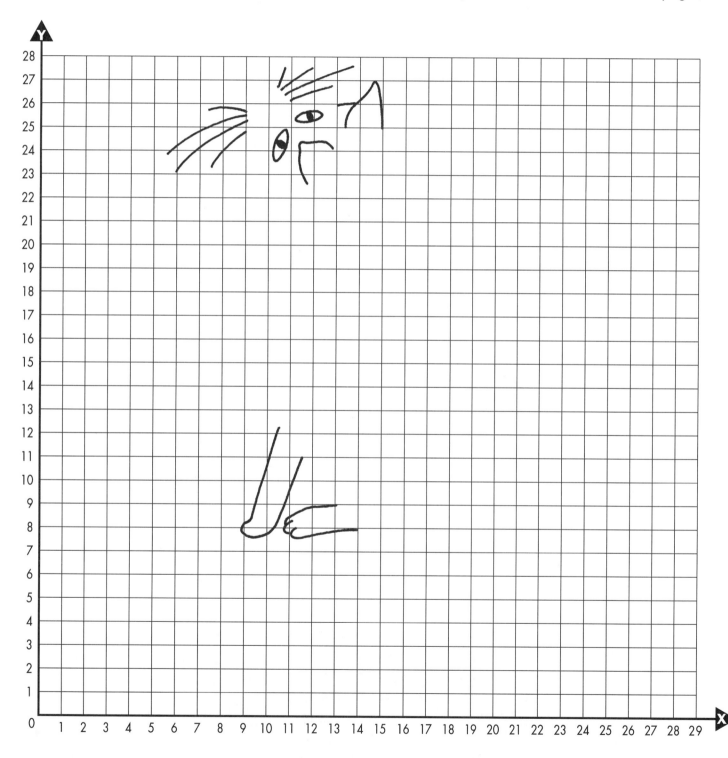

Mouse Trap

1. Look at number 1, below. The number in the first column is the X coordinate in an ordered pair.

2. On a separate sheet of paper, solve the problem in the second column. Write your answer on the blank line. The dollar amount in your answer is the Y coordinate.

3. Write the X and Y coordinates in the third column to make an ordered pair. The first one has been done for you.

4. Determine the ordered pairs for the rest of the chart.

5. Plot the ordered pairs on the graph on page 17 in the order they are given. Then use a straightedge to connect the points in the order you plotted them. Each time you come to the word "STOP," start a new line. Can you solve the riddle?

	X Coordinate	Y Coordinate	Ordered Pair
1.	8	$28.09 – $9.22 = $18.87 = $18	(8, 18)
2.	10	$35.47 – $13.30 = _____	STOP
3.	12	$33.49 – $12.45 = _____	
4.	10	$53.11 – $30.21 = _____	
5.	9	$55.90 – $31.15 = _____	
6.	9	$61.11 – $34.75 = _____	
7.	10	$44.12 – $17.02 = _____	
8.	11	$48.99 – $22.72 = _____	
9.	13	$50.13 – $23.68 = _____	
10.	15	$29.56 – $4.55 = _____	
11.	16	$25.09 – $1.32 = _____	
12.	14	$26.19 – $5.01 = _____	
13.	19	$40.45 – $25.30 = _____	
14.	21	$11.85 – $1.74 = _____	
15.	22	$15.97 – $8.94 = _____	
16.	27	$24.05 – $20.25 = _____	
17.	18	$9.51 – $7.06 = _____	
18.	24	$17.49 – $12.74 = _____	
19.	21	$34.10 – $27.15 = _____	
20.	13	$15.95 – $9.01 = _____	
21.	10	$11.30 – $5.90 = _____	
22.	10	$14.99 – $8.82 = _____	
23.	12	$9.74 – $2.70 = _____	
24.	18	$14.57 – $7.51 = _____	
25.	14	$16.29 – $7.41 = _____	
26.	10	$15.00 – $1.28 = _____	STOP
27.	11	$25.55 – $10.36 = _____	
28.	8	$15.91 – $9.38 = _____	
29.	5	$10.00 – $4.12 = _____	
30.	7	$10.97 – $3.11 = _____	
31.	9	24.47 – $9.12 = _____	
32.	8	$22.79 – $3.99 = _____	

Great Graph Art: Decimals and Fractions Scholastic Professional Books

Name_____

Rodeo

Why did the cowboy go to the rodeo when he was low on cash?_____

To find the answer, solve the problems on page 20. Then plot the ordered pairs and connect the points. The picture you make will help you solve the riddle. (The answer is upside down at the bottom of this page.)

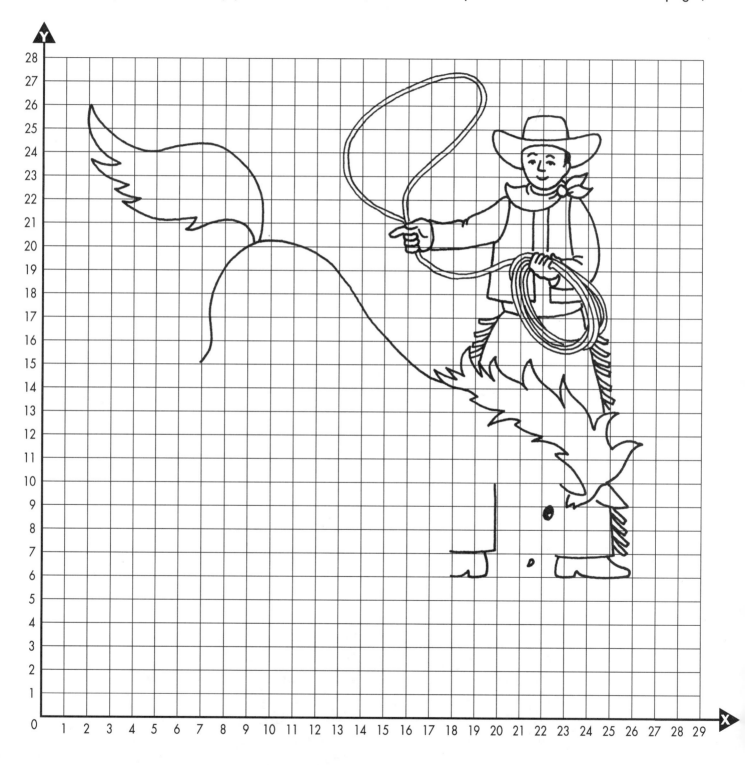

Answer: to get some bucks

Rodeo

1 Look at number 1, below. The number in the first column is the X coordinate in an ordered pair.

2 On a separate sheet of paper, solve the problem in the second column. Round the answer to the nearest whole number, and write it on the blank line. The whole number is the Y coordinate.

3 Write the X and Y coordinates in the third column to make an ordered pair. The first one has been done for you.

4 Determine the ordered pairs for the rest of the chart.

5 Plot the ordered pairs on the graph on page 19 in the order they are given. Then use a straightedge to connect the points in the order you plotted them. After you come to the word "STOP," start a new line. Can you solve the riddle?

	X Coordinate	Y Coordinate	Ordered Pair
1.	7	3.7 x 4 = 14.8 = 15	(7, 15)
2.	4	1.31 x 8 =	
3.	3	2.61 x 4 =	
4.	3	1.28 x 7 =	
5.	4	3.07 x 3 =	
6.	6	1.71 x 7 =	
7.	5	2.28 x 4 =	
8.	4	2.67 x 3 =	
9.	4	1.78 x 4 =	
10.	6	1.7 x 5 =	
11.	7	1.09 x 11 =	
12.	8	2.43 x 5 =	
13.	10	1.41 x 10 =	
14.	14	3.25 x 3 =	
15.	16	2.09 x 2 =	
16.	16	0.87 x 2 =	
17.	17	0.19 x 4 =	
18.	18	0.08 x 7 =	
19.	17	1.12 x 2 =	
20.	17	0.67 x 9 =	
21.	16	1.1 x 7 =	STOP
22.	17	0.78 x 8 =	
23.	19	1.19 x 2 =	
24.	20	0.44 x 5 =	
25.	18	2.11 x 3 =	
26.	18	3.79 x 2 =	
27.	20	1.24 x 8 =	
28.	22	1.14 x 9 =	
29.	21	1.47 x 6 =	
30.	21	2.89 x 2 =	
31.	22	3.09 x 2 =	
32.	25	1.12 x 9 =	

Great Graph Art: Decimals and Fractions Scholastic Professional Books

Name_____

Glowing Grin

What lights up a room with its grin on Halloween night? _____

To find the answer, solve the problems on page 22. Then plot the ordered pairs and connect the points. The picture you make will help you solve the riddle. (The answer is upside down at the bottom of this page.)

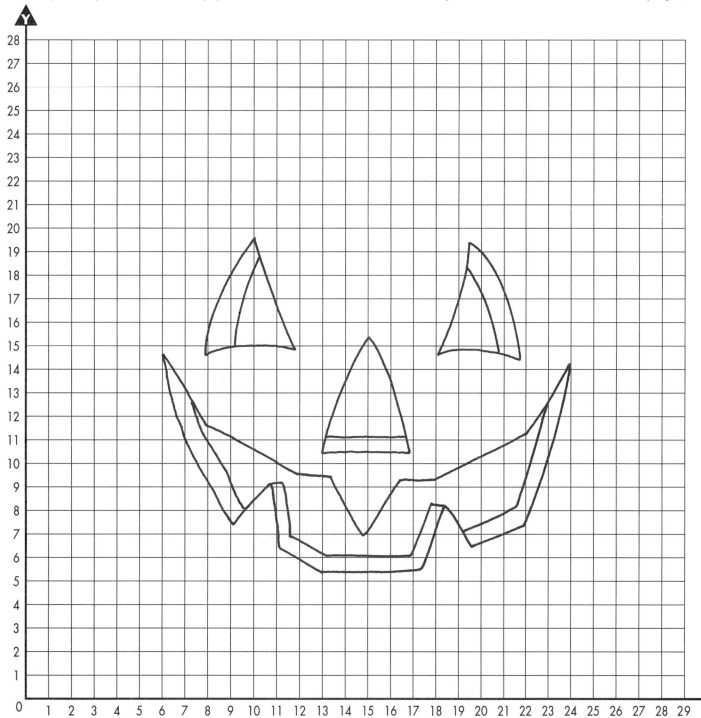

Answer: a jack-o-lantern

Name_____

Glowing Grin

1   Look at number 1, below. The number in the first column is the X coordinate in an ordered pair.

2   On a separate sheet of paper, solve the problem in the second column. Round the answer to the nearest whole number and write it on the blank line. The whole number is the Y coordinate.

3   Write the X and Y coordinates in the third column to make an ordered pair. The first one has been done for you.

4   Determine the ordered pairs for the rest of the chart.

5   Plot the ordered pairs on the graph on page 21 in the order they are given. Then use a straightedge to connect the points in the order you plotted them. Can you solve the riddle?

	X Coordinate	Y Coordinate	Ordered Pair
1.	18	$7.1 \times 3.5 =$ ___24.85 = 25___	(18, 25)
2.	17	$5.7 \times 4.4 =$ _____	
3.	16	$7.9 \times 2.9 =$ _____	
4.	16	$3.4 \times 6.3 =$ _____	
5.	19	$3.9 \times 5.6 =$ _____	
6.	22	$5.4 \times 4.1 =$ _____	
7.	25	$8.2 \times 2.4 =$ _____	
8.	27	$1.9 \times 8.2 =$ _____	
9.	27	$6.9 \times 1.3 =$ _____	
10.	26	$1.7 \times 3.4 =$ _____	
11.	24	$1.3 \times 3.4 =$ _____	
12.	22	$1.1 \times 1.5 =$ _____	
13.	18	$1.9 \times 0.7 =$ _____	
14.	12	$2.1 \times 0.4 =$ _____	
15.	8	$8.1 \times 0.2 =$ _____	
16.	6	$2.1 \times 1.7 =$ _____	
17.	4	$7.12 \times 0.8 =$ _____	
18.	3	$4.31 \times 2.1 =$ _____	
19.	3	$2.43 \times 6.6 =$ _____	
20.	5	$5.41 \times 3.7 =$ _____	
21.	8	$3.85 \times 5.7 =$ _____	
22.	11	$7.18 \times 3.1 =$ _____	
23.	14	$11.5 \times 1.8 =$ _____	
24.	13	$13.4 \times 1.7 =$ _____	
25.	15	$10.9 \times 2.4 =$ _____	
26.	17	$17.1 \times 1.6 =$ _____	
27.	18	$15.8 \times 1.58 =$ _____	

Great Graph Art: Decimals and Fractions Scholastic Professional Books

Name_____

New Job

Why did the dog trainer get a new job? _____

To find the answer, solve the problems on page 24. Then plot the ordered pairs and connect the points. The picture you make will help you solve the riddle. (The answer is upside down at the bottom of this page.)

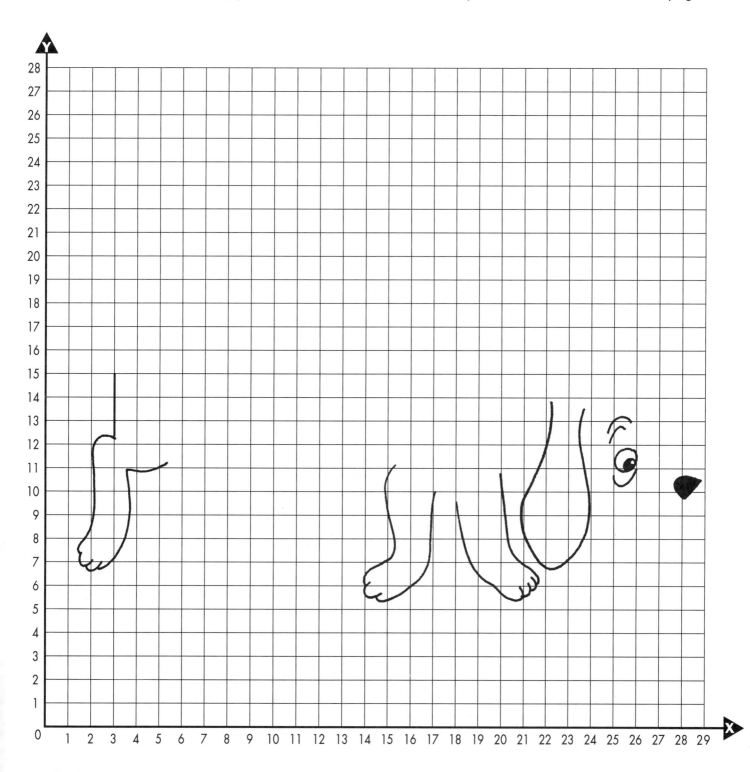

Answer: He was tired of being hounded.

New Job

1. Look at number 1, below. The number in the first column is the X coordinate in an ordered pair.

2. On a separate sheet of paper, solve the problem in the second column. Round the answer to the nearest whole number, and write it on the blank line. The whole number is the Y coordinate.

3. Write the X and Y coordinates in the third column to make an ordered pair. The first one has been done for you.

4. Determine the ordered pairs for the rest of the chart.

5. Plot the ordered pairs on the graph on page 23 in the order they are given. Then use a straightedge to connect the points in the order you plotted them. Each time you come to the word "STOP," start a new line. Can you solve the riddle?

	X Coordinate	Y Coordinate	Ordered Pair
1.	1	$75.9 \div 3 =$ ___25.3 = 25___	(1, 25)
2.	3	$77.6 \div 4 =$ _____	
3.	4	$35.8 \div 2 =$ _____	
4.	14	$69.6 \div 4 =$ _____	
5.	20	$86.5 \div 5 =$ _____	
6.	24	$65.2 \div 4 =$ _____	
7.	27	$88.9 \div 7 =$ _____	
8.	27	$74.4 \div 6 =$ _____	
9.	29	$39.6 \div 4 =$ _____	
10.	27	$24.6 \div 3 =$ _____	
11.	24	$60.9 \div 7 =$ _____	STOP
12.	21	$19.6 \div 2 =$ _____	
13.	20	$89.6 \div 8 =$ _____	
14.	17	$42.5 \div 5 =$ _____	STOP
15.	15	$56.4 \div 6 =$ _____	
16.	10	$77.7 \div 7 =$ _____	
17.	8	$24.2 \div 2 =$ _____	
18.	7	$37.6 \div 4 =$ _____	
19.	10	$19.8 \div 3 =$ _____	
20.	8	$53.1 \div 9 =$ _____	
21.	6	$58.8 \div 7 =$ _____	
22.	6	$82.4 \div 8 =$ _____	
23.	3	$29.4 \div 2 =$ _____	
24.	3	$51.3 \div 3 =$ _____	
25.	1	$73.6 \div 4 =$ _____	
26.	1	$49 \div 2 =$ _____	

Name_____

Take Off!

Why do astronauts want to study subtraction? _____

To find the answer, solve the problems on page 26. Then plot the ordered pairs and connect the points.
The picture you make will help you solve the riddle. (The answer is upside down at the bottom of this page.)

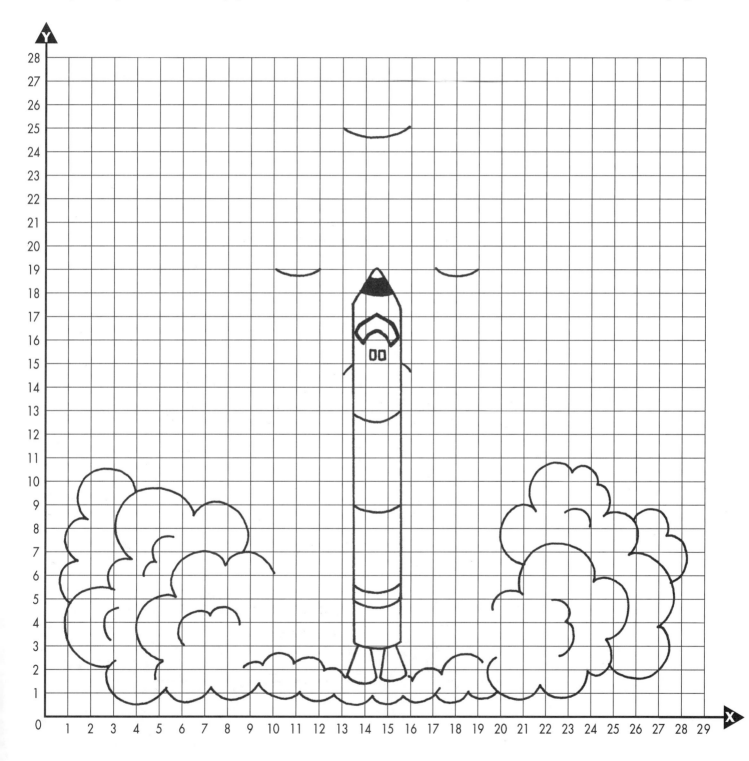

Answer: *They like to count down.*

Name_____

Division of Decimals by Decimals **0.1**

Take Off!

1. Look at number 1, below. The number in the first column is the X coordinate in an ordered pair.

2. On a separate sheet of paper, solve the problem in the second column. Round the answer to the nearest whole number, and write it on the blank line. The whole number is the Y coordinate.

3. Write the X and Y coordinates in the third column to make an ordered pair. The first one has been done for you.

4. Determine the ordered pairs for the rest of the chart.

5. Plot the ordered pairs on the graph on page 25 in the order they are given. Then use a straightedge to connect the points in the order you plotted them. Each time you come to the word "STOP," start a new line. Can you solve the riddle?

	X Coordinate	Y Coordinate	Ordered Pair
1.	21	$7.59 \div 2.3 =$ ___3.3 = 3___	(21, 3)
2.	16	$6.09 \div 2.1 =$ _____	
3.	16	$30.36 \div 1.2 =$ _____	
4.	15	$59.62 \div 2.2 =$ _____	
5.	14	$82.15 \div 3.1 =$ _____	
6.	13	$83.98 \div 3.4 =$ _____	
7.	13	$19.71 \div 7.3 =$ _____	
8.	8	$32.64 \div 9.6 =$ _____	
9.	10	$43.12 \div 8.8 =$ _____	
10.	10	$59.2 \div 3.2 =$ _____	
11.	11	$84.87 \div 4.1 =$ _____	
12.	12	$90.24 \div 4.7 =$ _____	
13.	12	$54.6 \div 8.4 =$ _____	STOP
14.	17	$68.82 \div 9.3 =$ _____	
15.	17	$99.32 \div 5.2 =$ _____	
16.	18	$56.97 \div 2.7 =$ _____	
17.	19	$75.66 \div 3.9 =$ _____	
18.	19	$52.92 \div 9.8 =$ _____	
19.	21	$28.13 \div 9.7 =$ _____	STOP
20.	10	$39.27 \div 7.7 =$ _____	
21.	12	$40.12 \div 5.9 =$ _____	
22.	13	$14.06 \div 1.9 =$ _____	STOP
23.	19	$36.57 \div 6.9 =$ _____	
24.	17	$71.28 \div 9.9 =$ _____	
25.	16	$32.43 \div 4.7 =$ _____	STOP

26

Name_____

Comparing and Ordering Fractions

Practice Makes Perfect

You know what they say: "Practice makes perfect." I have to practice my skills every day to stay on my toes. What am I? _____

To find the answer, solve the problems on page 28. Then plot the ordered pairs and connect the points. The picture you make will help you solve the riddle. (The answer is upside down at the bottom of this page.)

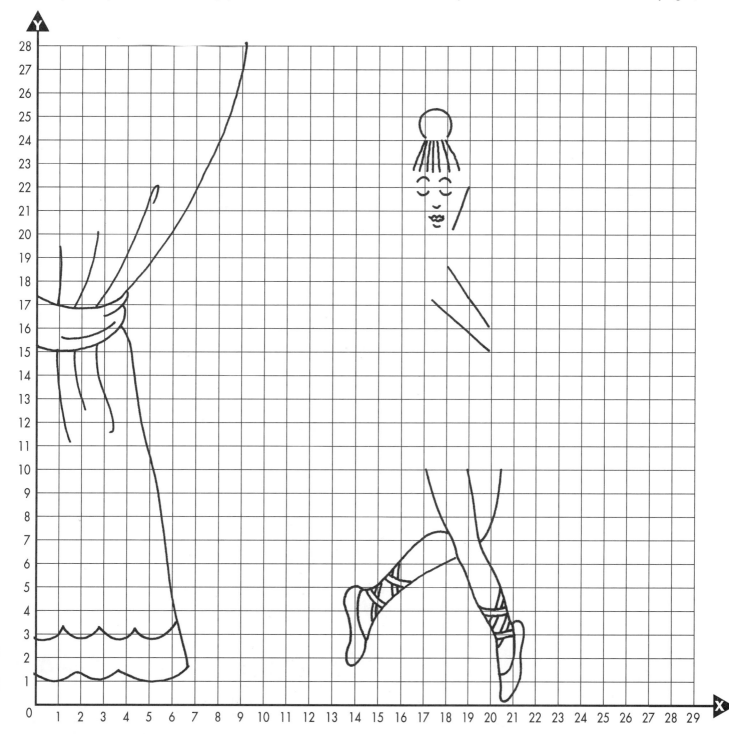

Answer: a ballerina

Great Graph Art: Decimals and Fractions   Scholastic Professional Books

27

Practice Makes Perfect

1. Look at number 1, right. The number in the first column is the X coordinate in an ordered pair.

2. Look at the fractions in the second column. Use < or > to compare the two fractions. The numerator of the largest number is the Y coordinate.

3. Write the X and Y coordinates in the third column to make an ordered pair. The first one has been done for you.

4. Determine the ordered pairs for the rest of the chart.

5. Plot the ordered pairs on the graph on page 27 in the order they are given. Then use a straightedge to connect the points in the order you plotted them. Can you solve the riddle?

	X Coordinate	Y Coordinate	Ordered Pair
1.	21	$\frac{13}{15} < \frac{28}{30}$	(21, 28)
2.	20	$\frac{26}{27}$ ___ $\frac{9}{10}$	
3.	20	$\frac{12}{17}$ ___ $\frac{22}{30}$	
4.	19	$\frac{9}{10}$ ___ $\frac{19}{20}$	
5.	20	$\frac{18}{20}$ ___ $\frac{7}{8}$	
6.	20	$\frac{6}{11}$ ___ $\frac{16}{20}$	
7.	24	$\frac{16}{24}$ ___ $\frac{4}{7}$	
8.	26	$\frac{14}{20}$ ___ $\frac{1}{2}$	
9.	24	$\frac{15}{18}$ ___ $\frac{4}{5}$	
10.	20	$\frac{3}{4}$ ___ $\frac{15}{16}$	
11.	24	$\frac{13}{25}$ ___ $\frac{1}{2}$	
12.	25	$\frac{11}{20}$ ___ $\frac{1}{2}$	
13.	23	$\frac{13}{17}$ ___ $\frac{11}{14}$	
14.	23	$\frac{10}{13}$ ___ $\frac{5}{9}$	
15.	15	$\frac{5}{6}$ ___ $\frac{10}{11}$	
16.	14	$\frac{1}{3}$ ___ $\frac{11}{15}$	
17.	13	$\frac{4}{9}$ ___ $\frac{11}{13}$	
18.	11	$\frac{13}{24}$ ___ $\frac{4}{9}$	
19.	11	$\frac{11}{13}$ ___ $\frac{14}{15}$	
20.	12	$\frac{14}{29}$ ___ $\frac{7}{15}$	
21.	12	$\frac{15}{30}$ ___ $\frac{4}{9}$	
22.	17	$\frac{3}{17}$ ___ $\frac{15}{19}$	
23.	17	$\frac{4}{13}$ ___ $\frac{16}{29}$	
24.	16	$\frac{18}{19}$ ___ $\frac{4}{5}$	
25.	17	$\frac{3}{7}$ ___ $\frac{20}{31}$	
26.	16	$\frac{22}{29}$ ___ $\frac{9}{15}$	
27.	17	$\frac{24}{31}$ ___ $\frac{2}{3}$	
28.	18	$\frac{24}{38}$ ___ $\frac{6}{13}$	
29.	19	$\frac{6}{11}$ ___ $\frac{22}{30}$	
30.	19	$\frac{27}{30}$ ___ $\frac{3}{5}$	
31.	21	$\frac{1}{7}$ ___ $\frac{28}{60}$	

Great Graph Art: Decimals and Fractions Scholastic Professional Books

Name_____

Solar System

What is the smartest member of the solar system? _____

To find the answer, solve the problems on page 30. Then plot the ordered pairs and connect the points. The picture you make will help you solve the riddle. (The answer is upside down at the bottom of this page.)

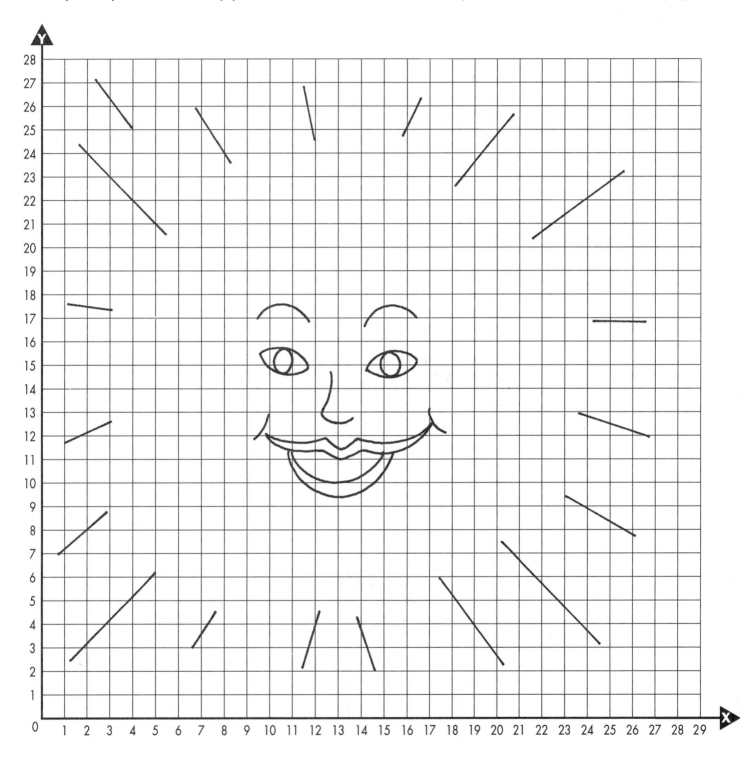

Answer: The sun is the brightest.

Equivalent Fractions

Solar System

1 Look at number 1, left. The number in the first column is the X coordinate in an ordered pair.

2 Look at the numbers in the second column. Write the missing number so that the fractions are equivalent. The missing number is the Y coordinate.

3 Write the X and Y coordinates in the third column to make an ordered pair. The first one has been done for you.

4 Determine the ordered pairs for the rest of the chart.

5 Plot the ordered pairs on the graph on page 29 in the order they are given. Then use a straightedge to connect the points in the order you plotted them. Can you solve the riddle?

	X Coordinate	Y Coordinate	Ordered Pair
1.	14	$\frac{4}{9} = \frac{12}{27}$	(14, 27)
2.	15	$\frac{3}{7} = \frac{9}{}$	
3.	17	$\frac{6}{9} = \frac{}{36}$	
4.	17	$\frac{2}{3} = \frac{}{30}$	
5.	22	$\frac{1}{2} = \frac{}{46}$	
6.	19	$\frac{2}{6} = \frac{6}{}$	
7.	25	$\frac{1}{3} = \frac{}{57}$	
8.	20	$\frac{1}{8} = \frac{2}{}$	
9.	26	$\frac{2}{9} = \frac{}{63}$	
10.	21	$\frac{1}{10} = \frac{}{130}$	
11.	25	$\frac{2}{5} = \frac{4}{}$	
12.	20	$\frac{1}{5} = \frac{}{55}$	
13.	25	$\frac{2}{11} = \frac{}{33}$	
14.	19	$\frac{2}{3} = \frac{6}{}$	
15.	20	$\frac{1}{5} = \frac{}{25}$	
16.	17	$\frac{1}{7} = \frac{}{49}$	
17.	17	$\frac{1}{44} = \frac{}{88}$	
18.	13	$\frac{2}{3} = \frac{4}{}$	
19.	9	$\frac{1}{7} = \frac{}{14}$	
20.	10	$\frac{1}{12} = \frac{}{84}$	
21.	7	$\frac{1}{19} = \frac{}{95}$	
22.	8	$\frac{1}{4} = \frac{2}{}$	
23.	3	$\frac{2}{2} = \frac{6}{}$	
24.	7	$\frac{1}{9} = \frac{}{99}$	
25.	3	$\frac{2}{5} = \frac{4}{}$	
26.	6	$\frac{1}{7} = \frac{}{91}$	
27.	1	$\frac{3}{7} = \frac{6}{}$	
28.	6	$\frac{3}{8} = \frac{6}{}$	
29.	3	$\frac{1}{5} = \frac{}{95}$	
30.	8	$\frac{2}{3} = \frac{12}{}$	
31.	5	$\frac{1}{7} = \frac{}{161}$	
32.	10	$\frac{9}{10} = \frac{18}{}$	
33.	10	$\frac{11}{12} = \frac{22}{}$	
34.	12	$\frac{2}{3} = \frac{14}{}$	
35.	14	$\frac{9}{15} = \frac{}{45}$	

Great Graph Art: Decimals and Fractions   Scholastic Professional Books

Name_____

Flower Shop

Why did the bicyclist go to the flower shop?_____

To find the answer, solve the problems on page 32. Then plot the ordered pairs and connect the points.
The picture you make will help you solve the riddle. (The answer is upside down at the bottom of this page.)

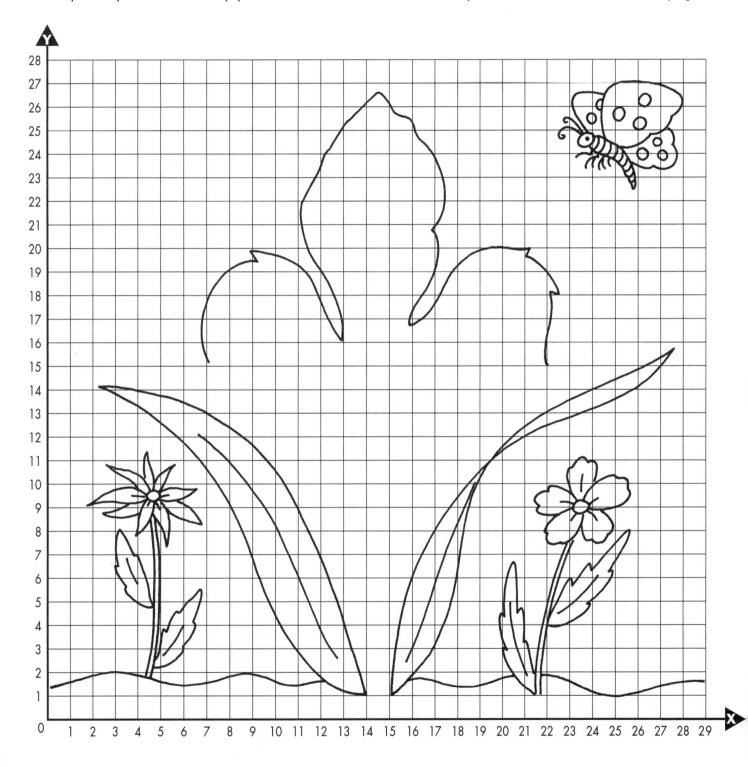

Answer: He needed new petals (pedals).

Great Graph Art: Decimals and Fractions Scholastic Professional Books

31

Flower Shop

1. Look at number 1, right. The number in the first column is the X coordinate in an ordered pair.

2. Rename the fraction in the second column in its lowest terms. The new numerator is the Y coordinate.

3. Write the X and Y coordinates in the third column to make an ordered pair. The first one has been done for you.

4. Determine the ordered pairs for the rest of the chart.

5. Plot the ordered pairs on the graph on page 31 in the order they are given. Then use a straightedge to connect the points in the order you plotted them. After you come to the word "STOP," start a new line.

	X Coordinate	Y Coordinate	Ordered Pair
1.	15	$\frac{9}{81} = \frac{1}{9}$	(15, 1)
2.	15	$\frac{36}{51} =$	
3.	17	$\frac{52}{68} =$	
4.	19	$\frac{54}{57} =$	
5.	22	$\frac{45}{66} =$	
6.	23	$\frac{32}{82} =$	
7.	23	$\frac{90}{235} =$	
8.	24	$\frac{40}{194} =$	
9.	22	$\frac{69}{90} =$	
10.	21	$\frac{46}{100} =$	
11.	20	$\frac{52}{178} =$	
12.	19	$\frac{78}{87} =$	
13.	17	$\frac{48}{106} =$	STOP
14.	12	$\frac{96}{124} =$	
15.	10	$\frac{52}{142} =$	
16.	9	$\frac{78}{129} =$	
17.	8	$\frac{46}{122} =$	
18.	7	$\frac{92}{364} =$	
19.	5	$\frac{60}{81} =$	
20.	6	$\frac{54}{75} =$	
21.	6	$\frac{48}{69} =$	
22.	7	$\frac{30}{44} =$	
23.	10	$\frac{36}{70} =$	
24.	12	$\frac{52}{68} =$	
25.	14	$\frac{48}{76} =$	
26.	14	$\frac{18}{144} =$	

Name_____

Vacation

What animal is always ready to go on vacation? _____

To find the answer, solve the problems on page 34. Then plot the ordered pairs and connect the points. The picture you make will help you solve the riddle. (The answer is upside down at the bottom of this page.)

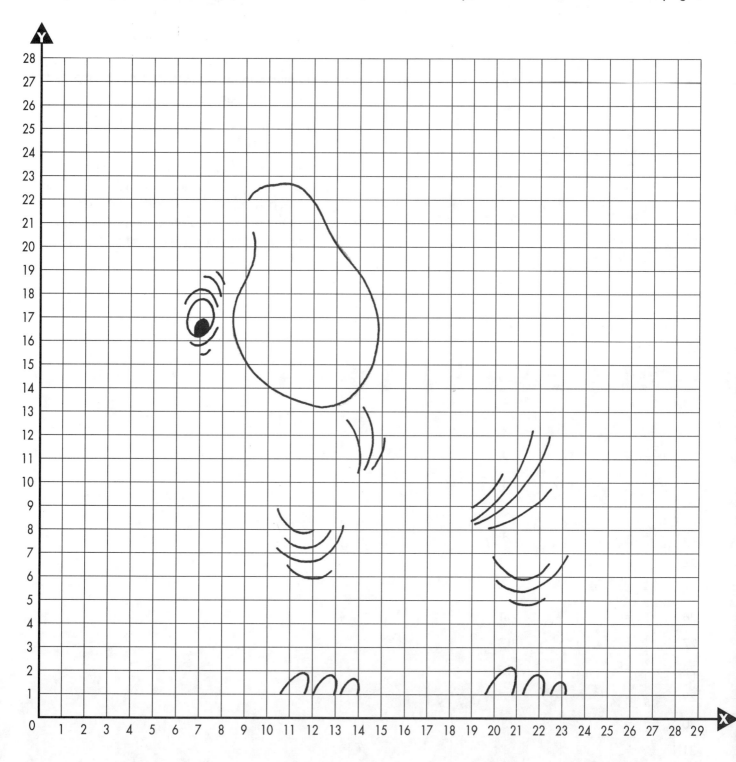

Answer: An elephant! It always has its trunk with it.

	X Coordinate	Y Coordinate	Ordered Pair
1.	$\frac{34}{19}$ = 1$\frac{15}{19}$	1	(15, 1)
2.	$\frac{48}{17}$ =	10	
3.	$\frac{79}{20}$ =	8	
4.	$\frac{93}{24}$ =	3	
5.	$\frac{40}{21}$ =	1	
6.	$\frac{74}{25}$ =	1	
7.	$\frac{54}{30}$ =	8	
8.	$\frac{53}{27}$ =	12	
9.	$\frac{85}{29}$ =	9	
10.	$\frac{59}{33}$ =	18	
11.	$\frac{123}{25}$ =	23	
12.	$\frac{62}{43}$ =	24	
13.	$\frac{100}{17}$ =	24	
14.	$\frac{108}{16}$ =	22	STOP
15.	$\frac{99}{10}$ =	22	
16.	$\frac{62}{8}$ =	22	
17.	$\frac{29}{5}$ =	20	
18.	$\frac{21}{6}$ =	8	
19.	$\frac{45}{8}$ =	2	
20.	$\frac{77}{10}$ =	2	
21.	$\frac{18}{11}$ =	3	
22.	$\frac{60}{9}$ =	3	
23.	$\frac{53}{7}$ =	8	
24.	$\frac{35}{6}$ =	12	
25.	$\frac{54}{8}$ =	10	
26.	$\frac{78}{8}$ =	11	
27.	$\frac{34}{13}$ =	13	
28.	$\frac{19}{10}$ =	13	
29.	$\frac{70}{15}$ =	7	
30.	$\frac{40}{14}$ =	3	
31.	$\frac{32}{22}$ =	1	
32.	$\frac{34}{19}$ =	1	

Vacation

1 Look at number 1, left. Write the improper fraction in the first column as a mixed fraction. Do not rename the fraction in lowest terms. The new numerator is the X coordinate. The Y coordinate is given.

2 Write the X and Y coordinates in the third column to make an ordered pair. The first one has been done for you.

3 Determine the ordered pairs for the rest of the chart.

4 Plot the ordered pairs on the graph on page 33 in the order they are given. Then use a straightedge to connect the points in the order you plotted them. After you come to the word "STOP," start a new line. Can you solve the riddle?

Name_____

Ship's Friend

What works best when it's at the end of its rope?_____

To find the answer, solve the problems on page 36. Then plot the ordered pairs and connect the points. The picture you make will help you solve the riddle. (The answer is upside down at the bottom of this page.)

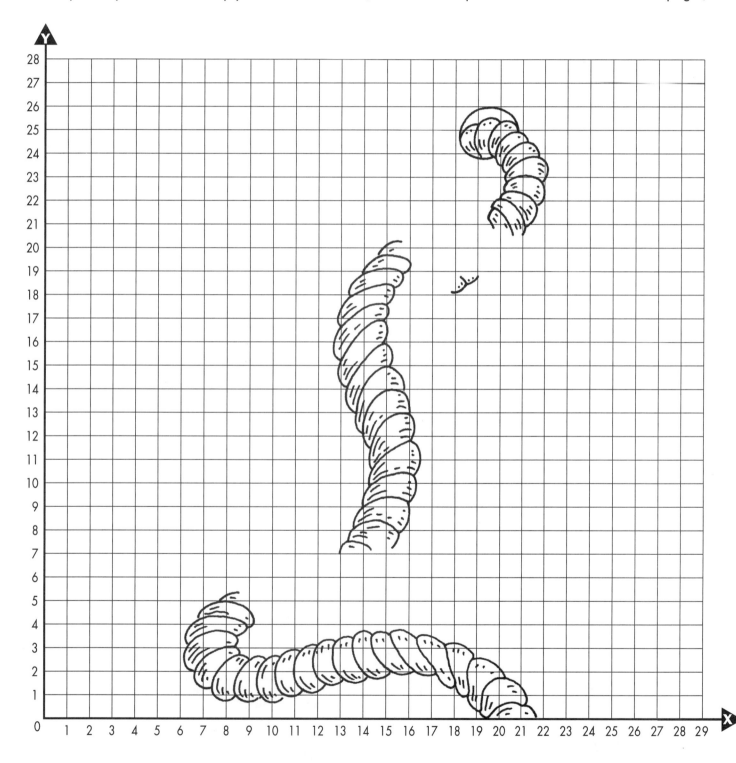

Answer: an anchor

Great Graph Art: Decimals and Fractions   Scholastic Professional Books

35

Name_____

Mixed Numbers to Improper Fractions

Ship's Friend

	X Coordinate	Y Coordinate	Ordered Pair
1.	10	$1\frac{1}{2} = \frac{3}{2}$	(10, 3)
2.	22	$2\frac{1}{3} =$	
3.	23	$1\frac{2}{3} =$	
4.	25	$2\frac{1}{4} =$	
5.	20	$4\frac{1}{2} =$	
6.	22	$2\frac{2}{3} =$	
7.	13	$3\frac{1}{2} =$	STOP
8.	16	$4\frac{2}{3} =$	
9.	18	$6\frac{1}{3} =$	
10.	22	$4\frac{3}{4} =$	
11.	23	$3\frac{2}{6} =$	
12.	19	$4\frac{1}{5} =$	
13.	20	$3\frac{2}{7} =$	STOP
14.	22	$4\frac{4}{5} =$	
15.	22	$5\frac{1}{5} =$	
16.	20	$3\frac{6}{7} =$	
17.	19	$3\frac{3}{8} =$	
18.	17	$3\frac{5}{7} =$	
19.	17	$3\frac{3}{7} =$	
20.	18	$7\frac{2}{3} =$	
21.	17	$5\frac{2}{4} =$	
22.	14	$3\frac{2}{7} =$	
23.	13	$3\frac{1}{7} =$	
24.	16	$2\frac{2}{9} =$	
25.	16	$4\frac{3}{4} =$	STOP
26.	13	$2\frac{2}{6} =$	
27.	10	$2\frac{2}{3} =$	
28.	5	$6\frac{1}{2} =$	
29.	7	$2\frac{3}{5} =$	
30.	3	$3\frac{1}{5} =$	
31.	2	$1\frac{3}{9} =$	
32.	4	$3\frac{1}{4} =$	
33.	10	$1\frac{1}{2} =$	

1. Look at number 1, left. The number in the first column is the X coordinate in an ordered pair.

2. Look at the second column. Write the mixed fraction as an improper fraction. The numerator will be the Y coordinate.

3. Write the X and Y coordinates in the third column to make an ordered pair. The first one has been done for you.

4. Plot the ordered pairs on the graph on page 35 in the order they are given. Then use a straightedge to connect the points in the order you plotted them. Each time you come to the word "STOP," start a new line. Can you solve the riddle?

36

Great Graph Art: Decimals and Fractions Scholastic Professional Books

Name_____

Ice Cream Parlor

After weeks of rain, why did the weatherperson go to the ice cream parlor? _____

To find the answer, solve the problems on page 38. Then plot the ordered pairs and connect the points. The picture you make will help you solve the riddle. (The answer is upside down at the bottom of this page.)

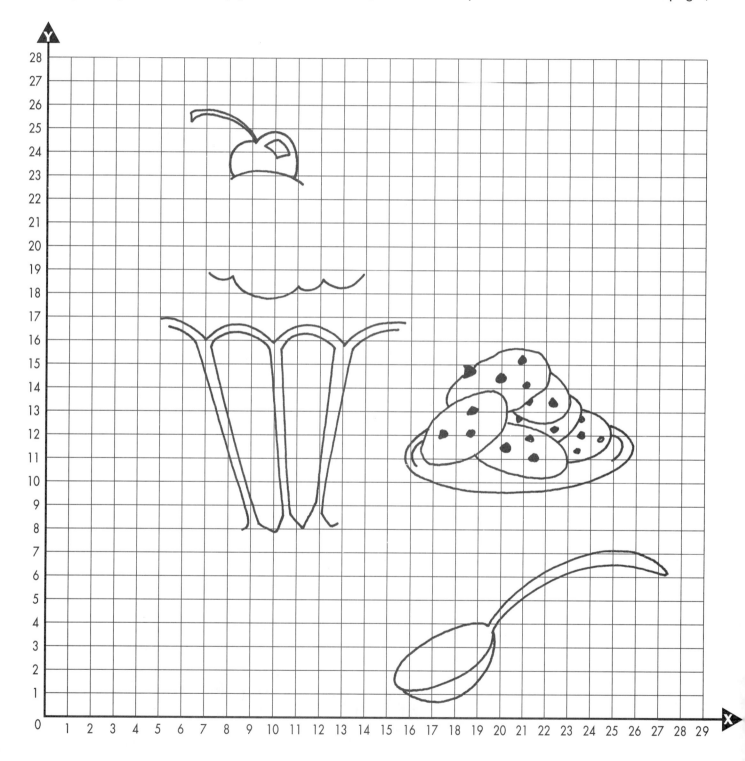

Answer: She wanted a "sun" day (sundae).

Ice Cream Parlor

1. Look at number 1, right. The number in the first column is the X coordinate in an ordered pair.

2. On a separate sheet of paper, solve the problem in the second column. Rename the answer in lowest terms. The numerator in the answer is the Y coordinate.

3. Write the X and Y coordinates in the third column to make an ordered pair. The first one has been done for you.

4. Determine the ordered pairs for the rest of the chart.

5. Plot the ordered pairs on the graph on page 37 in the order they are given. Then use a straightedge to connect the points in the order you plotted them. Each time you come to the word "STOP," start a new line. Can you solve the riddle?

	X Coordinate	Y Coordinate	Ordered Pair
1.	5	$\frac{9}{20} + \frac{8}{20} = \frac{17}{20}$	(5, 17)
2.	8	$\frac{8}{34} + \frac{8}{34} =$	
3.	10	$\frac{6}{9} + \frac{1}{9} =$	
4.	9	$\frac{5}{22} + \frac{7}{22} =$	
5.	5	$\frac{8}{15} + \frac{4}{15} =$	
6.	6	$\frac{4}{38} + \frac{2}{38} =$	
7.	9	$\frac{3}{14} + \frac{1}{14} =$	
8.	12	$\frac{3}{27} + \frac{3}{27} =$	
9.	15	$\frac{2}{7} + \frac{1}{7} =$	
10.	16	$\frac{3}{25} + \frac{17}{25} =$	
11.	12	$\frac{4}{13} + \frac{2}{13} =$	
12.	11	$\frac{15}{60} + \frac{13}{60} =$	
13.	13	$\frac{3}{17} + \frac{5}{17} =$	
14.	16	$\frac{6}{19} + \frac{11}{19} =$	STOP
15.	15	$\frac{5}{40} + \frac{29}{40} =$	
16.	15	$\frac{12}{19} + \frac{6}{19} =$	
17.	14	$\frac{11}{91} + \frac{8}{91} =$	
18.	15	$\frac{13}{29} + \frac{7}{29} =$	
19.	14	$\frac{14}{47} + \frac{7}{47} =$	
20.	14	$\frac{19}{46} + \frac{25}{46} =$	
21.	13	$\frac{11}{30} + \frac{12}{30} =$	
22.	11	$\frac{28}{120} + \frac{41}{120} =$	STOP
23.	8	$\frac{9}{25} + \frac{14}{25} =$	
24.	7	$\frac{19}{27} + \frac{3}{27} =$	
25.	7	$\frac{18}{58} + \frac{24}{58} =$	
26.	6	$\frac{5}{43} + \frac{15}{43} =$	
27.	7	$\frac{18}{20} + \frac{1}{20} =$	
28.	6	$\frac{23}{69} + \frac{31}{69} =$	
29.	6	$\frac{5}{20} + \frac{12}{20} =$	

Great Graph Art: Decimals and Fractions   Scholastic Professional Books

Name_____

What Am I?

What has hands but no feet,
A face but no nose,
No mouth, but demands an answer?_____

To find the answer, solve the problems on page 40. Then plot the ordered pairs and connect the points.
The picture you make will help you solve the riddle. (The answer is upside down at the bottom of this page.)

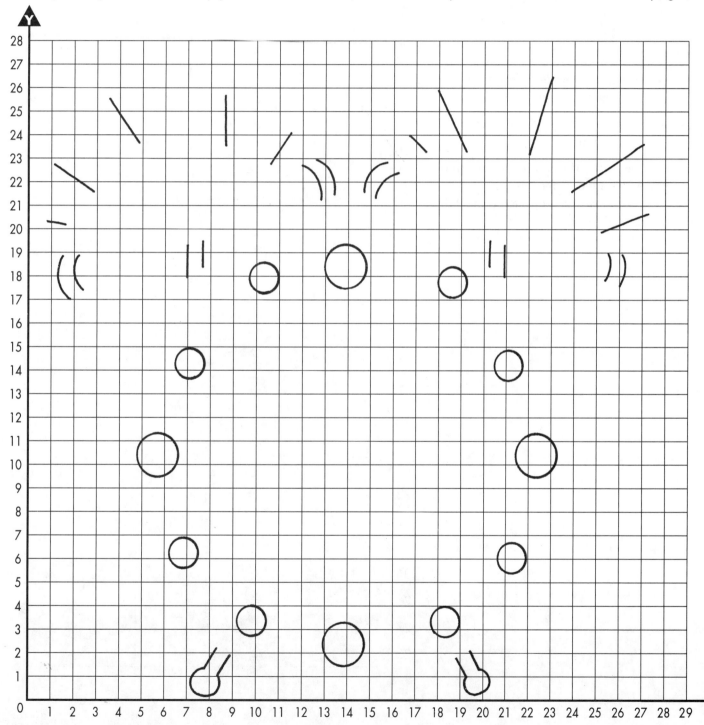

Answer: an alarm clock

Name_____

What Am I?

1. Look at number 1, right. The number in the first column is the X coordinate in an ordered pair.

2. On a separate sheet of paper, solve the problem in the second column. Rename the answer in lowest terms. The numerator in the answer is the Y coordinate.

3. Write the X and Y coordinates in the third column to make an ordered pair. The first one has been done for you.

4. Determine the ordered pairs for the rest of the chart.

5. Plot the ordered pairs on the graph on page 39 in the order they are given. Then use a straightedge to connect the points in the order you plotted them. Each time you come to the word "STOP," start a new line. Can you solve the riddle?

	X Coordinate	Y Coordinate	Ordered Pair
1.	11	$\frac{29}{21} - \frac{9}{21} = \frac{20}{21}$	(11, 20)
2.	17	$\frac{35}{83} - \frac{15}{83} =$	
3.	21	$\frac{22}{23} - \frac{4}{23} =$	
4.	24	$\frac{29}{30} - \frac{3}{30} =$	
5.	24	$\frac{12}{17} - \frac{4}{17} =$	
6.	21	$\frac{8}{38} - \frac{2}{38} =$	
7.	17	$\frac{9}{21} - \frac{6}{21} =$	
8.	11	$\frac{13}{20} - \frac{8}{20} =$	
9.	7	$\frac{10}{11} - \frac{7}{11} =$	
10.	4	$\frac{35}{36} - \frac{3}{36} =$	
11.	4	$\frac{16}{17} - \frac{3}{17} =$	
12.	7	$\frac{23}{25} - \frac{5}{25} =$	
13.	11	$\frac{45}{62} - \frac{5}{62} =$	STOP
14.	14	$\frac{30}{35} - \frac{2}{35} =$	
15.	14	$\frac{27}{34} - \frac{5}{34} =$	
16.	19	$\frac{19}{17} - \frac{3}{17} =$	STOP
17.	17	$\frac{27}{29} - \frac{5}{29} =$	
18.	22	$\frac{31}{37} - \frac{9}{37} =$	
19.	25	$\frac{39}{40} - \frac{1}{40} =$	
20.	25	$\frac{22}{25} - \frac{4}{25} =$	
21.	16	$\frac{44}{40} - \frac{23}{40} =$	
22.	17	$\frac{41}{53} - \frac{19}{53} =$	STOP
23.	11	$\frac{78}{93} - \frac{12}{93} =$	
24.	12	$\frac{25}{26} - \frac{4}{26} =$	
25.	3	$\frac{22}{23} - \frac{4}{23} =$	
26.	3	$\frac{62}{58} - \frac{24}{58} =$	
27.	6	$\frac{41}{43} - \frac{19}{43} =$	
28.	11	$\frac{28}{29} - \frac{6}{29} =$	

Great Graph Art: Decimals and Fractions Scholastic Professional Books

Name_____

Lost Job

Why did the amphibian lose his job? _____

To find the answer, solve the problems on page 42. Then plot the ordered pairs and connect the points. The picture you make will help you solve the riddle. (The answer is upside down at the bottom of this page.)

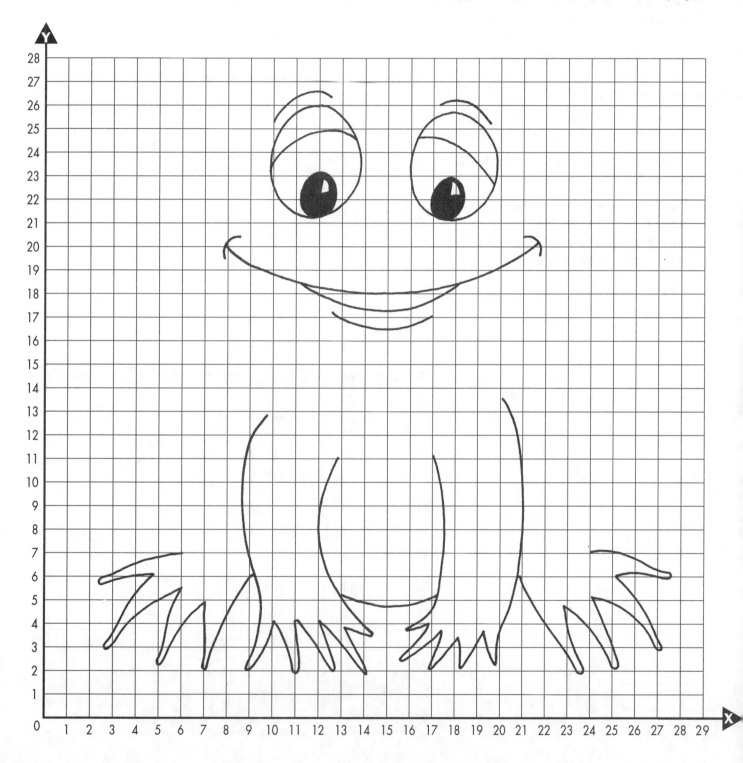

Answer: *He was the low man on the totem (toad-em) pole.*

Lost Job

1 Look at number 1, right. The number in the first column is the X coordinate in an ordered pair.

2 On a separate sheet of paper, solve the problem in the second column. Rename the answer in lowest terms. The numerator in the answer is the Y coordinate.

3 Write the X and Y coordinates in the third column to make an ordered pair. The first one has been done for you.

4 Determine the ordered pairs for the rest of the chart.

5 Plot the ordered pairs on the graph on page 41 in the order they are given. Then use a straightedge to connect the points in the order you plotted them. Each time you come to the word "STOP," start a new line. Can you solve the riddle?

	X Coordinate	Y Coordinate	Ordered Pair
1.	6	$\frac{2}{10} + \frac{3}{20} = \frac{7}{20}$	(6, 7)
2.	3	$\frac{3}{30} + \frac{5}{6} =$	
3.	4	$\frac{4}{5} + \frac{2}{40} =$	
4.	5	$\frac{6}{22} + \frac{1}{2} =$	
5.	9	$\frac{7}{38} + \frac{17}{38} =$	STOP
6.	9	$\frac{1}{7} + \frac{1}{35} =$	
7.	6	$\frac{1}{2} + \frac{3}{7} =$	STOP
8.	24	$\frac{1}{5} + \frac{4}{15} =$	
9.	27	$\frac{9}{25} + \frac{1}{5} =$	
10.	26	$\frac{1}{4} + \frac{3}{5} =$	
11.	25	$\frac{4}{9} + \frac{9}{18} =$	
12.	21	$\frac{10}{26} + \frac{7}{13} =$	STOP
13.	24	$\frac{1}{3} + \frac{2}{7} =$	
14.	21	$\frac{1}{25} + \frac{1}{5} =$	STOP
15.	24	$\frac{1}{3} + \frac{7}{27} =$	
16.	22	$\frac{2}{5} + \frac{9}{20} =$	
17.	23	$\frac{2}{27} + \frac{2}{3} =$	
18.	21	$\frac{2}{5} + \frac{12}{25} =$	
19.	22	$\frac{28}{58} + \frac{10}{29} =$	
20.	19	$\frac{15}{40} + \frac{6}{20} =$	
21.	17	$\frac{5}{29} + \frac{44}{58} =$	
22.	15	$\frac{3}{8} + \frac{13}{32} =$	
23.	13	$\frac{2}{5} + \frac{11}{40} =$	
24.	11	$\frac{7}{37} + \frac{20}{37} =$	
25.	8	$\frac{11}{29} + \frac{13}{29} =$	
26.	9	$\frac{3}{5} + \frac{7}{25} =$	
27.	7	$\frac{17}{23} + \frac{9}{69} =$	
28.	8	$\frac{2}{25} + \frac{3}{5} =$	
29.	6	$\frac{2}{7} + \frac{6}{35} =$	

Great Graph Art: Decimals and Fractions   Scholastic Professional Books

Name_____

Boating

What kind of boat do you buy when you're short on cash? _____

To find the answer, solve the problems on page 44. Then plot the ordered pairs and connect the points.
The picture you make will help you solve the riddle. (The answer is upside down at the bottom of this page.)

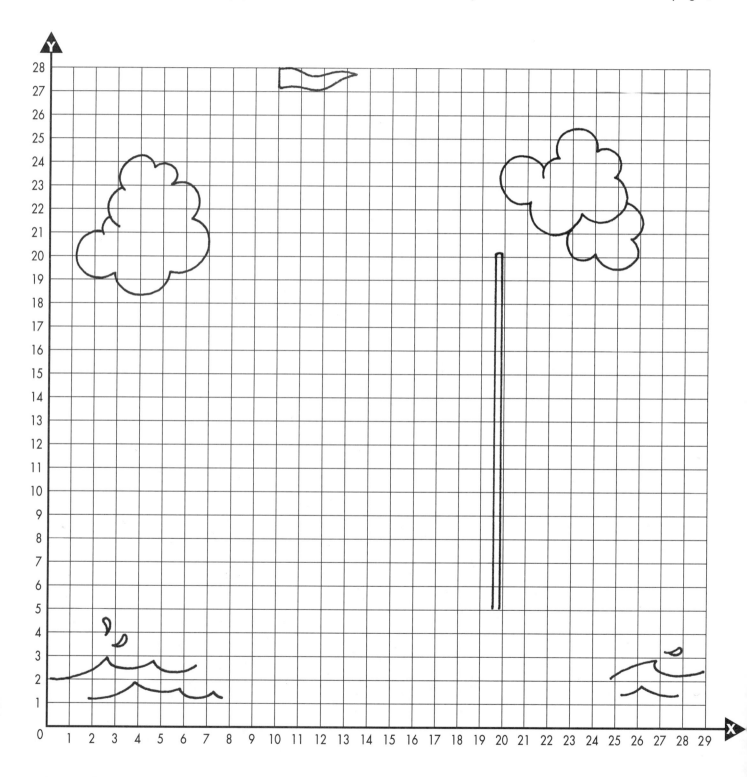

Name_____

Boating

1 Look at number 1, below. The number in the first column is the X coordinate in an ordered pair.

2 On a separate sheet of paper, solve the problem in the second column. Rename the answer in lowest terms. The numerator in the answer is the Y coordinate.

3 Write the X and Y coordinates in the third column to make an ordered pair. The first one has been done for you.

4 Determine the ordered pairs for the rest of the chart.

5 Plot the ordered pairs on the graph on page 43 in the order they are given. Then use a straightedge to connect the points in the order you plotted them. Each time you come to the word "STOP," start a new line. Can you solve the riddle?

	X Coordinate	Y Coordinate	Ordered Pair
1.	4	$\frac{11}{12} - \frac{2}{4} = \frac{5}{12}$	(4, 5)
2.	27	$\frac{15}{19} - \frac{20}{38} =$	
3.	24	$\frac{22}{33} - \frac{1}{3} =$	
4.	8	$\frac{24}{27} - \frac{7}{9} =$	
5.	4	$\frac{6}{7} - \frac{13}{21} =$	STOP
6.	4	$\frac{10}{11} - \frac{8}{22} =$	
7.	9	$\frac{50}{50} - \frac{3}{25} =$	
8.	9	$\frac{27}{35} - \frac{3}{5} =$	
9.	4	$\frac{12}{19} - \frac{12}{38} =$	STOP
10.	10	$\frac{7}{9} - \frac{9}{18} =$	
11.	10	$\frac{7}{8} - \frac{1}{32} =$	
12.	15	$\frac{6}{7} - \frac{1}{28} =$	
13.	10	$\frac{34}{34} - \frac{1}{17} =$	STOP
14.	10	$\frac{2}{5} - \frac{16}{55} =$	
15.	19	$\frac{1}{5} - \frac{7}{65} =$	
16.	16	$\frac{26}{27} - \frac{1}{9} =$	
17.	10	$\frac{27}{32} - \frac{3}{8} =$	STOP
18.	20	$\frac{33}{35} - \frac{6}{70} =$	
19.	26	$\frac{14}{26} - \frac{6}{78} =$	
20.	21	$\frac{11}{20} - \frac{3}{40} =$	
21.	20	$\frac{25}{28} - \frac{3}{14} =$	

Great Graph Art: Decimals and Fractions Scholastic Professional Books

Name_____

Addition of Mixed Fractions With Like Denominators

World Wide Web

What creature works on the World Wide Web? _____

To find the answer, solve the problems on page 46. Then plot the ordered pairs and connect the points. The picture you make will help you solve the riddle. (The answer is upside down at the bottom of this page.)

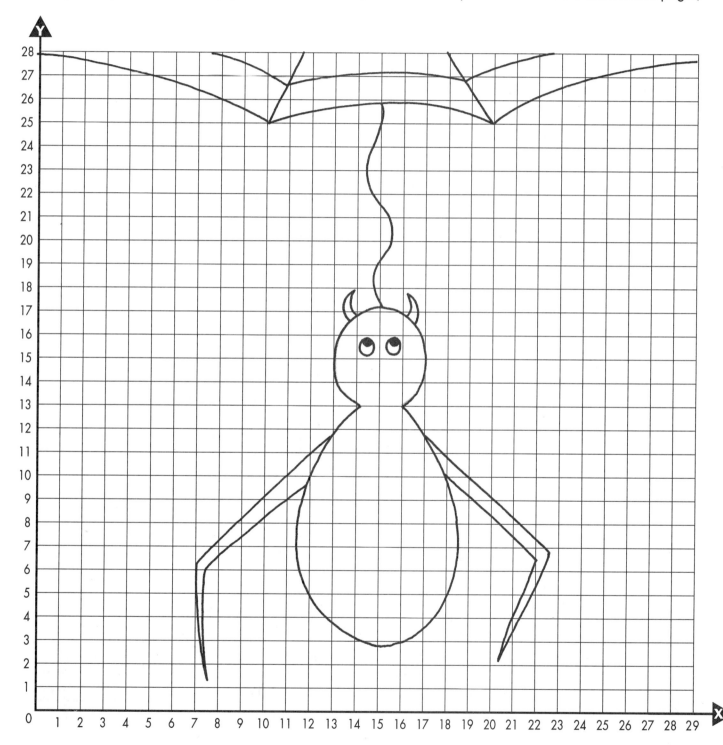

Great Graph Art: Decimals and Fractions Scholastic Professional Books

World Wide Web

1. Look at number 1, right. The number in the first column is the X coordinate in an ordered pair.

2. On a separate sheet of paper, solve the problem in the second column. Rename the answer in lowest terms. The numerator in the answer is the Y coordinate.

3. Write the X and Y coordinates in the third column to make an ordered pair. The first one has been done for you.

4. Determine the ordered pairs for the rest of the chart.

5. Plot the ordered pairs on the graph on page 45 in the order they are given. Then use a straightedge to connect the points in the order you plotted them. Each time you come to the word "STOP," start a new line. Can you solve the riddle?

	X Coordinate	Y Coordinate	Ordered Pair
1.	17	$3\frac{5}{17} + 4\frac{11}{17} = 7\frac{16}{17}$	(17, 16)
2.	21	$7\frac{9}{23} + 6\frac{11}{23} =$	
3.	20	$1\frac{23}{29} + 3\frac{2}{29} =$	
4.	22	$2\frac{13}{27} + 5\frac{7}{27} =$	
5.	17	$6\frac{9}{19} + 3\frac{6}{19} =$	STOP
6.	17	$2\frac{8}{27} + 5\frac{6}{27} =$	
7.	24	$5\frac{7}{31} + 1\frac{8}{31} =$	
8.	28	$1\frac{13}{20} + 1\frac{6}{20} =$	
9.	24	$5\frac{7}{15} + 1\frac{7}{15} =$	
10.	16	$3\frac{19}{30} + 4\frac{7}{30} =$	
11.	22	$4\frac{15}{34} + 4\frac{7}{34} =$	
12.	25	$2\frac{13}{35} + 3\frac{17}{35} =$	
13.	22	$6\frac{4}{11} + 6\frac{6}{11} =$	
14.	17	$2\frac{5}{37} + 1\frac{7}{37} =$	STOP
15.	13	$1\frac{2}{21} + 2\frac{14}{21} =$	
16.	9	$7\frac{13}{31} + 9\frac{7}{31} =$	
17.	10	$13\frac{18}{51} + 5\frac{7}{51} =$	
18.	8	$3\frac{19}{29} + 4\frac{1}{29} =$	
19.	13	$4\frac{15}{34} + 5\frac{15}{34} =$	STOP
20.	13	$7\frac{7}{27} + 22\frac{7}{27} =$	
21.	6	$2\frac{6}{53} + 6\frac{9}{53} =$	
22.	2	$6\frac{15}{40} + 5\frac{23}{40} =$	
23.	6	$15\frac{6}{18} + 6\frac{8}{18} =$	
24.	14	$1\frac{16}{51} + 4\frac{23}{51} =$	
25.	7	$7\frac{13}{32} + 5\frac{9}{32} =$	
26.	4	$6\frac{5}{46} + 1\frac{7}{46} =$	
27.	7	$8\frac{1}{57} + 8\frac{9}{57} =$	
28.	13	$6\frac{5}{35} + 13\frac{7}{35} =$	

Great Graph Art: Decimals and Fractions Scholastic Professional Books

Name_____

Bad Habits

Why don't fish smoke cigarettes?_____

To find the answer, solve the problems on page 48. Then plot the ordered pairs and connect the points. The picture you make will help you solve the riddle. (The answer is upside down at the bottom of this page.)

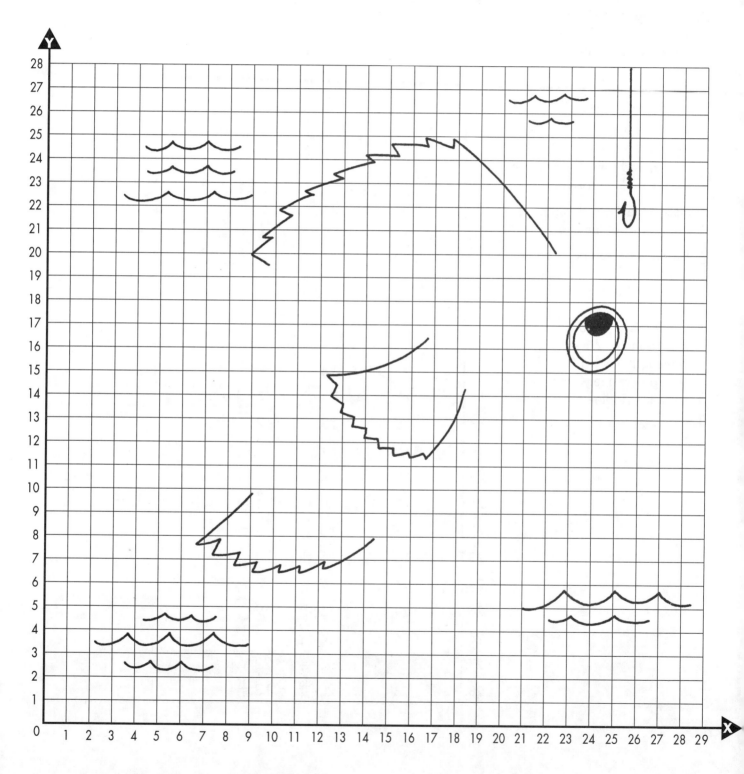

Answer: They are afraid that they'll get hooked.

Great Graph Art: Decimals and Fractions Scholastic Professional Books

Bad Habits

1. Look at number 1, right. The number in the first column is the X coordinate in an ordered pair.

2. On a separate sheet of paper, solve the problem in the second column. Rename the answer in lowest terms. The numerator in the answer is the Y coordinate.

3. Write the X and Y coordinates in the third column to make an ordered pair. The first one has been done for you.

4. Determine the ordered pairs for the rest of the chart.

5. Plot the ordered pairs on the graph on page 47 in the order they are given. Then use a straightedge to connect the points in the order you plotted them. When you come to the word "STOP," start a new line. Can you solve the riddle?

	X Coordinate	Y Coordinate	Ordered Pair
1.	28	$12\frac{25}{57} - 5\frac{9}{57} = 7\frac{16}{57}$	(28, 16)
2.	25	$17\frac{22}{23} - 6\frac{3}{23} =$	
3.	17	$9\frac{29}{31} - 3\frac{7}{31} =$	
4.	15	$12\frac{24}{25} - 5\frac{2}{25} =$	
5.	10	$15\frac{35}{51} - 6\frac{15}{51} =$	
6.	8	$9\frac{33}{34} - 5\frac{1}{34} =$	
7.	5	$5\frac{38}{47} - 2\frac{22}{47} =$	
8.	3	$11\frac{33}{39} - 3\frac{13}{39} =$	
9.	1	$7\frac{27}{29} - 1\frac{9}{29} =$	
10.	2	$24\frac{37}{38} - 7\frac{7}{38} =$	
11.	2	$13\frac{19}{33} - 5\frac{5}{33} =$	
12.	1	$5\frac{38}{52} - 3\frac{16}{52} =$	
13.	3	$16\frac{18}{32} - 7\frac{9}{32} =$	
14.	5	$12\frac{45}{37} - 9\frac{32}{37} =$	
15.	8	$9\frac{34}{45} - 2\frac{21}{45} =$	
16.	8	$14\frac{30}{34} - 9\frac{8}{34} =$	
17.	11	$33\frac{37}{39} - 14\frac{13}{39} =$	
18.	15	$13\frac{19}{31} - 2\frac{11}{31} =$	
19.	15	$14\frac{35}{84} - 5\frac{19}{84} =$	
20.	19	$17\frac{10}{11} - 3\frac{2}{11} =$	STOP
21.	17	$12\frac{19}{23} - 4\frac{13}{23} =$	
22.	17	$16\frac{15}{42} - 6\frac{7}{42} =$	
23.	20	$15\frac{16}{19} - 13\frac{8}{19} =$	
24.	24	$9\frac{16}{51} - 4\frac{7}{51} =$	
25.	28	$15\frac{45}{58} - 9\frac{21}{58} =$	
26.	26	$6\frac{27}{31} - 4\frac{14}{31} =$	
27.	27	$35\frac{16}{17} - 22\frac{2}{17} =$	
28.	28	$20\frac{26}{71} - 13\frac{10}{71} =$	

Great Graph Art: Decimals and Fractions   Scholastic Professional Books

Shoemaker

Why did the shoemaker quit her job? _____

To find the answer, solve the problems on page 50. Then plot the ordered pairs and connect the points. The picture you make will help you solve the riddle. (Thse answer is upside down at the bottom of this page.)

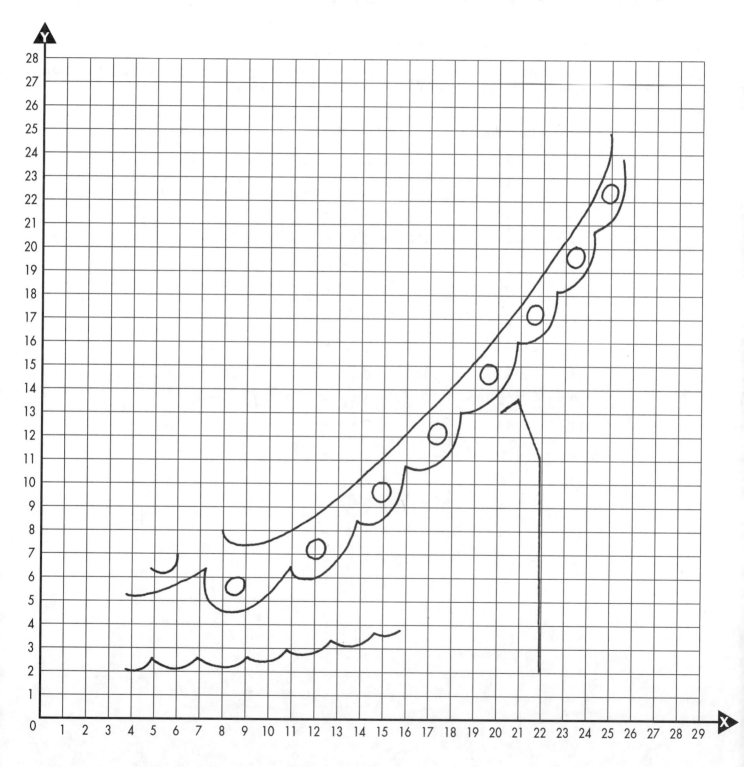

Answer: *She was tired of working with heels.*

Shoemaker

1 Look at number 1, below. The number in the first column is the X coordinate in an ordered pair.

2 On a separate sheet of paper, solve the problem in the second column. Rename the answer in lowest terms. The numerator in the answer is the Y coordinate.

3 Write the X and Y coordinates in the third column to make an ordered pair. The first one has been done for you.

4 Determine the ordered pairs for the rest of the chart.

5 Plot the ordered pairs on the graph on page 49 in the order they are given. Then use a straightedge to connect the points in the order you plotted them. Can you solve the riddle?

	X Coordinate	Y Coordinate	Ordered Pair
1.	24	$3\frac{16}{27} + 2\frac{1}{3} = 5\frac{25}{27}$	(24, 25)
2.	25	$7\frac{5}{32} + 4\frac{5}{8} =$	
3.	27	$6\frac{3}{5} + 3\frac{6}{25} =$	
4.	27	$2\frac{3}{15} + 2\frac{11}{30} =$	
5.	24	$6\frac{10}{36} + 2\frac{6}{18} =$	
6.	24	$1\frac{1}{5} + 1\frac{2}{10} =$	
7.	22	$5\frac{2}{18} + 1\frac{1}{9} =$	
8.	21	$1\frac{1}{8} + 2\frac{1}{4} =$	
9.	21	$1\frac{6}{38} + 4\frac{7}{19} =$	
10.	20	$3\frac{18}{42} + 4\frac{7}{14} =$	
11.	15	$4\frac{2}{30} + 2\frac{1}{15} =$	
12.	8	$1\frac{4}{9} + 1\frac{1}{18} =$	
13.	4	$7\frac{2}{7} + 7\frac{3}{14} =$	
14.	3	$2\frac{1}{9} + 3\frac{1}{3} =$	
15.	4	$2\frac{6}{14} + 1\frac{3}{7} =$	
16.	8	$8\frac{3}{25} + 9\frac{1}{5} =$	
17.	24	$11\frac{22}{82} + 8\frac{14}{41} =$	

Name_____

Zoo Friends

Which animal in the zoo never stands up for its friends when they are in trouble?

_____

To find the answer, solve the problems on page 52. Then plot the ordered pairs and connect the points. The picture you make will help you solve the riddle. (The answer is upside down at the bottom of this page.)

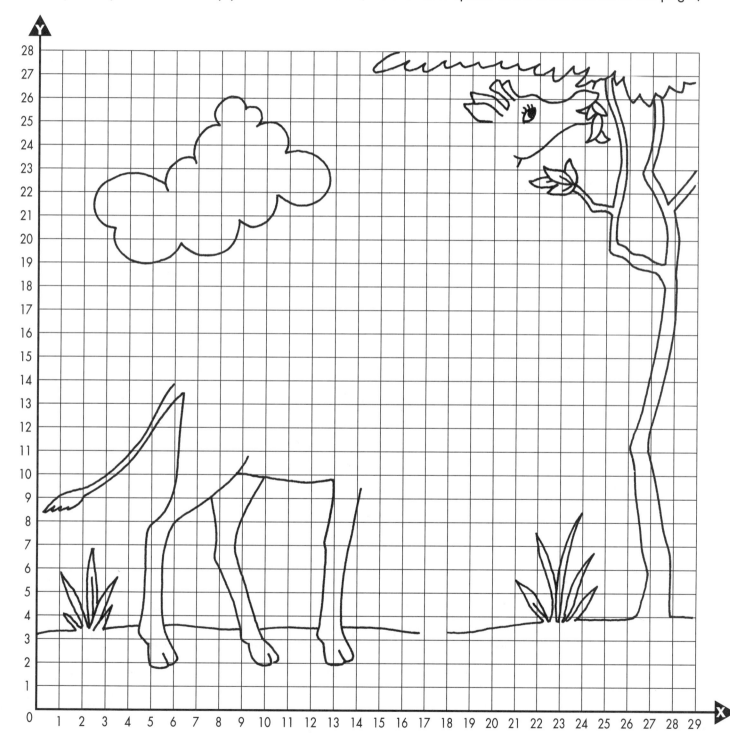

Answer: A giraffe. It's tired of sticking its neck out.

Name_____

Zoo Friends

1 Look at number 1, below. The number in the first column is the X coordinate in an ordered pair.

2 On a separate sheet of paper, solve the problem in the second column. Rename the answer in lowest terms. The denominator in the answer is the Y coordinate.

3 Write the X and Y coordinates in the third column to make an ordered pair. The first one has been done for you.

4 Determine the ordered pairs for the rest of the chart.

5 Plot the ordered pairs on the graph on page 51 in the order they are given. Then use a straightedge to connect the points in the order you plotted them. When you come to the word "STOP," start a new line. Can you solve the riddle?

	X Coordinate	Y Coordinate	Ordered Pair
1.	6	$8\frac{4}{7} - 2\frac{1}{2} = 6\frac{1}{14}$	(6, 14)
2.	7	$6\frac{4}{6} - 5\frac{1}{5} =$	
3.	11	$7\frac{9}{16} - 3\frac{1}{4} =$	
4.	13	$9\frac{7}{9} - 2\frac{1}{2} =$	
5.	15	$8\frac{8}{19} - 7\frac{2}{38} =$	
6.	17	$4\frac{2}{3} - 1\frac{4}{21} =$	
7.	20	$3\frac{11}{25} - 1\frac{1}{5} =$	STOP
8.	21	$5\frac{8}{46} - 4\frac{1}{23} =$	
9.	19	$2\frac{12}{57} - 2\frac{1}{19} =$	
10.	16	$9\frac{3}{7} - 8\frac{3}{14} =$	
11.	16	$6\frac{2}{4} - 3\frac{1}{8} =$	
12.	17	$7\frac{8}{12} - 5\frac{1}{2} =$	
13.	18	$9\frac{8}{18} - 9\frac{1}{9} =$	
14.	19	$6\frac{5}{9} - 1\frac{1}{18} =$	
15.	18	$5 \quad - 2\frac{1}{2} =$	
16.	17	$4 \quad - 2\frac{1}{3} =$	
17.	16	$3\frac{10}{12} - 2\frac{4}{6} =$	
18.	14	$8\frac{9}{10} - 1\frac{1}{5} =$	
19.	13	$11\frac{9}{10} - 2\frac{4}{5} =$	

Great Graph Art: Decimals and Fractions Scholastic Professional Books

Name_____

Giant Fish

What do you call a giant fish that never misses its target?_____

To find the answer, solve the problems on page 54. Then plot the ordered pairs and connect the points. The picture you make will help you solve the riddle. (The answer is upside down at the bottom of this page.)

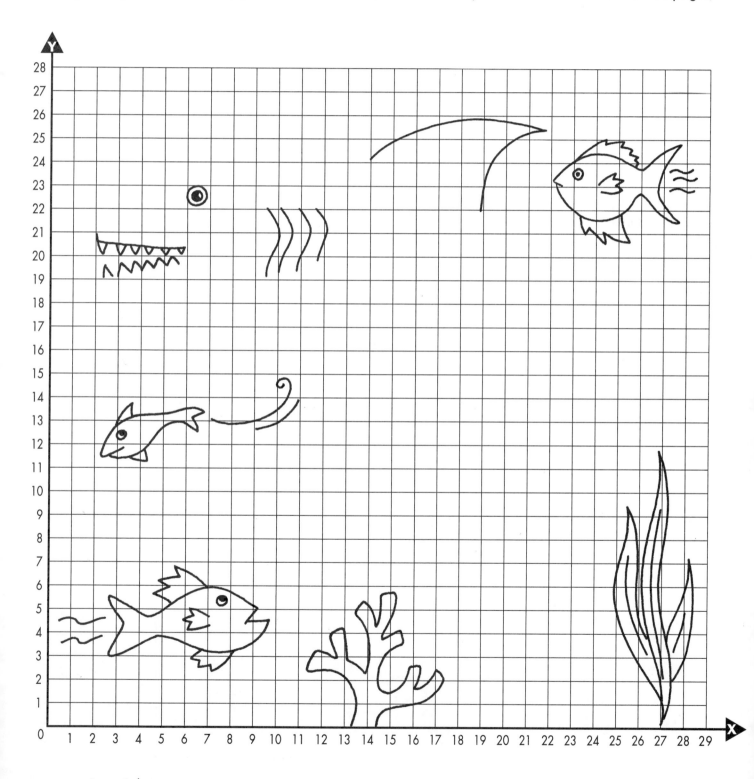

Name_____

Giant Fish

1. Look at number 1, right. The number in the first column is the X coordinate in an ordered pair.

2. On a separate sheet of paper, solve the problem in the second column. Rename the answer in lowest terms. The numerator in the answer is the Y coordinate.

3. Write the X and Y coordinates in the third column to make an ordered pair. The first one has been done for you.

4. Determine the ordered pairs for the rest of the chart.

5. Plot the ordered pairs on the graph on page 53 in the order they are given. Then use a straightedge to connect the points in the order you plotted them. Can you solve the riddle?

	X Coordinate	Y Coordinate	Ordered Pair
1.	8	$\frac{5}{7} \times \frac{4}{7} = \frac{20}{49}$	(8, 20)
2.	2	$\frac{7}{10} \times \frac{3}{4} =$	
3.	1	$\frac{11}{13} \times \frac{2}{5} =$	
4.	4	$\frac{6}{11} \times \frac{4}{5} =$	
5.	9	$\frac{5}{7} \times \frac{5}{9} =$	
6.	14	$\frac{2}{5} \times \frac{12}{13} =$	
7.	23	$\frac{4}{9} \times \frac{5}{9} =$	
8.	26	$\frac{4}{3} \times \frac{4}{9} =$	
9.	26	$\frac{1}{5} \times \frac{13}{9} =$	
10.	25	$\frac{5}{17} \times \frac{2}{1} =$	
11.	22	$\frac{1}{3} \times \frac{7}{12} =$	
12.	26	$\frac{5}{6} \times \frac{3}{5} =$	
13.	17	$\frac{3}{1} \times \frac{2}{17} =$	
14.	17	$\frac{1}{19} \times \frac{7}{1} =$	
15.	15	$\frac{3}{2} \times \frac{7}{12} =$	
16.	11	$\frac{9}{11} \times \frac{2}{2} =$	
17.	6	$\frac{5}{7} \times \frac{2}{7} =$	
18.	10	$\frac{11}{3} \times \frac{3}{28} =$	
19.	16	$\frac{4}{13} \times \frac{5}{2} =$	
20.	19	$\frac{9}{10} \times \frac{4}{4} =$	
21.	21	$\frac{2}{7} \times \frac{5}{13} =$	
22.	21	$\frac{6}{17} \times \frac{4}{2} =$	
23.	18	$\frac{3}{8} \times \frac{5}{7} =$	
24.	12	$\frac{17}{1} \times \frac{1}{19} =$	
25.	10	$\frac{2}{10} \times \frac{17}{5} =$	
26.	7	$\frac{5}{8} \times \frac{3}{8} =$	
27.	8	$\frac{17}{12} \times \frac{3}{5} =$	
28.	3	$\frac{9}{5} \times \frac{2}{5} =$	
29.	2	$\frac{38}{4} \times \frac{2}{20} =$	
30.	8	$\frac{5}{11} \times \frac{4}{11} =$	

Great Graph Art: Decimals and Fractions Scholastic Professional Books

Name_____

Mystery Bear

What kind of bear never eats food but is always stuffed? _____

To find the answer, solve the problems on page 56. Then plot the ordered pairs and connect the points.
The picture you make will help you solve the riddle. (The answer is upside down at the bottom of this page.)

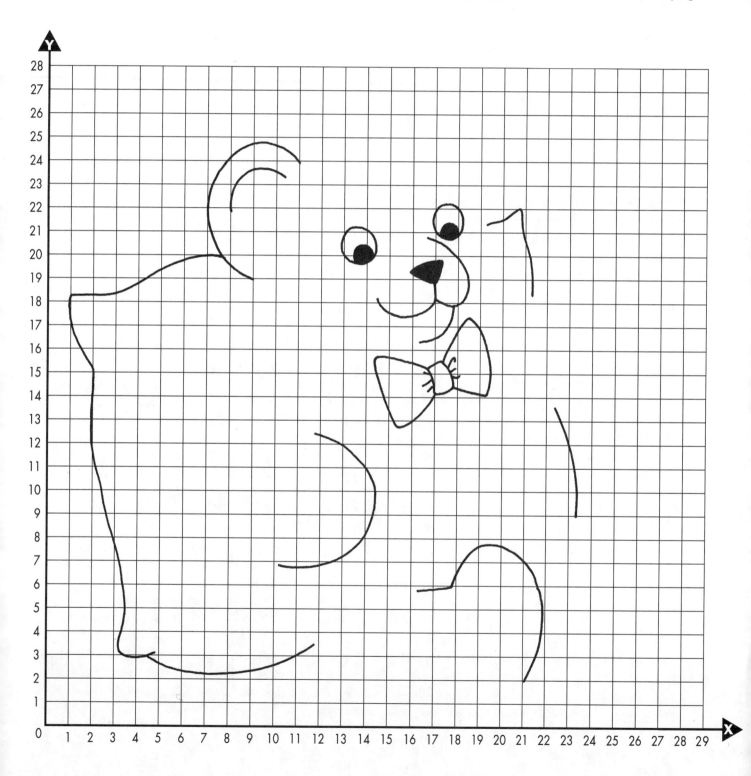

Mystery Bear

1. Look at number 1, right. The number in the first column is the X coordinate in an ordered pair.

2. On a separate sheet of paper, solve the problem in the second column. Rename the answer in lowest terms. The numerator in the answer is the Y coordinate.

3. Write the X and Y coordinates in the third column to make an ordered pair. The first one has been done for you.

4. Determine the ordered pairs for the rest of the chart.

5. Plot the ordered pairs on the graph on page 55 in the order they are given. Then use a straightedge to connect the points in the order you plotted them When you come to the word "STOP," start a new line. Can you solve the riddle?

	X Coordinate	Y Coordinate	Ordered Pair
1.	11	$6 \times \frac{4}{25} = \frac{24}{25}$	(11, 24)
2.	16	$5 \times \frac{5}{29} =$	
3.	17	$\frac{13}{29} \times 2 =$	
4.	19	$\frac{26}{62} \times 2 =$	
5.	20	$\frac{5}{27} \times 5 =$	
6.	20	$23 \times \frac{1}{28} =$	
7.	19	$\frac{11}{81} \times 2 =$	
8.	20	$\frac{1}{20} \times 19 =$	
9.	19	$17 \times \frac{1}{45} =$	
10.	21	$\frac{9}{19} \times 2 =$	
11.	22	$1 \times \frac{19}{30} =$	
12.	23	$19 \times \frac{2}{60} =$	
13.	25	$17 \times \frac{2}{40} =$	
14.	25	$5 \times \frac{3}{19} =$	
15.	21	$\frac{1}{24} \times 13 =$	
16.	23	$9 \times \frac{5}{50} =$	
17.	25	$\frac{6}{64} \times 6 =$	
18.	28	$2 \times \frac{5}{22} =$	
19.	25	$6 \times \frac{4}{40} =$	
20.	22	$\frac{5}{49} \times 7 =$	STOP
21.	21	$2 \times \frac{2}{6} =$	
22.	15	$1 \times \frac{1}{34} =$	
23.	10	$\frac{5}{9} \times 1 =$	
24.	10	$7 \times \frac{1}{12} =$	
25.	8	$2 \times \frac{9}{20} =$	
26.	8	$3 \times \frac{4}{13} =$	
27.	10	$\frac{8}{19} \times 2 =$	
28.	9	$19 \times \frac{1}{25} =$	

Great Graph Art: Decimals and Fractions   Scholastic Professional Books

Name_____

Pierre the Great

How did Pierre the Penguin know he was destined for greatness? _____

To find the answer, solve the problems on page 58. Then plot the ordered pairs and connect the points. The picture you make will help you solve the riddle. (The answer is upside down at the bottom of this page.)

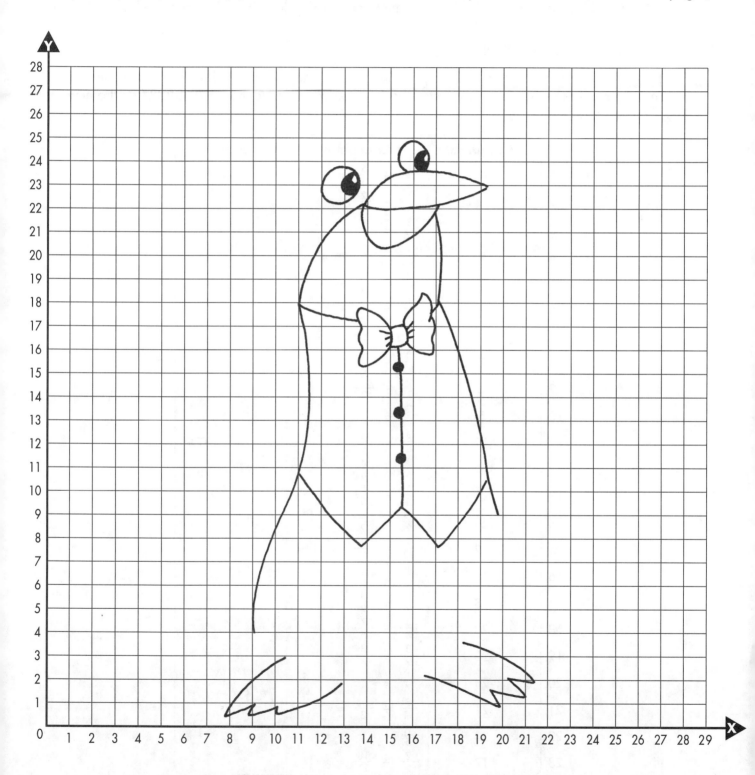

Answer: He was born wearing a tuxedo.

Great Graph Art: Decimals and Fractions Scholastic Professional Books

Pierre the Great

1. Look at number 1, below. The number in the first column is the X coordinate in an ordered pair.

2. On a separate sheet of paper, solve the problem in the second column. Rename the answer in lowest terms. The denominator in the answer is the Y coordinate.

3. Write the X and Y coordinates in the third column to make an ordered pair. The first one has been done for you.

4. Determine the ordered pairs for the rest of the chart.

5. Plot the ordered pairs on the graph on page 57 in the order they are given. Then use a straightedge to connect the points in the order you plotted them. When you come to the word "STOP," start a new line. Can you solve the riddle?

	X Coordinate	Y Coordinate	Ordered Pair
1.	16	$\frac{1}{5} \div \frac{5}{3} = \frac{3}{25}$	(16, 25)
2.	14	$\frac{1}{13} \div \frac{2}{11} =$	
3.	12	$\frac{3}{26} \div \frac{1}{7} =$	
4.	9	$\frac{1}{12} \div \frac{2}{11} =$	
5.	8	$\frac{3}{2} \div \frac{11}{3} =$	
6.	9	$\frac{1}{4} \div \frac{5}{19} =$	
7.	11	$\frac{9}{1} \div \frac{3}{6} =$	
8.	7	$\frac{2}{13} \div \frac{1}{3} =$	
9.	4	$\frac{2}{7} \div \frac{1}{2} =$	
10.	5	$\frac{2}{3} \div \frac{7}{9} =$	
11.	10	$\frac{4}{8} \div \frac{6}{5} =$	STOP
12.	8	$\frac{3}{5} \div \frac{4}{6} =$	
13.	5	$\frac{3}{6} \div \frac{5}{5} =$	
14.	9	$\frac{3}{9} \div \frac{4}{9} =$	
15.	12	$\frac{1}{17} \div \frac{2}{17} =$	
16.	16	$\frac{1}{5} \div \frac{2}{5} =$	
17.	18	$\frac{2}{9} \div \frac{3}{9} =$	
18.	20	$\frac{4}{4} \div \frac{7}{5} =$	
19.	20	$\frac{8}{9} \div \frac{8}{4} =$	
20.	24	$\frac{1}{7} \div \frac{1}{5} =$	
21.	21	$\frac{3}{11} \div \frac{1}{3} =$	
22.	20	$\frac{2}{5} \div \frac{3}{7} =$	
23.	17	$\frac{2}{2} \div \frac{18}{11} =$	

Great Graph Art: Decimals and Fractions Scholastic Professional Books

Name_____

Banker

Why does Dixie the Duck want to be a banker when she grows up?_____

To find the answer, solve the problems on page 60. Then plot the ordered pairs and connect the points. The picture you make will help you solve the riddle. (The answer is upside down at the bottom of this page.)

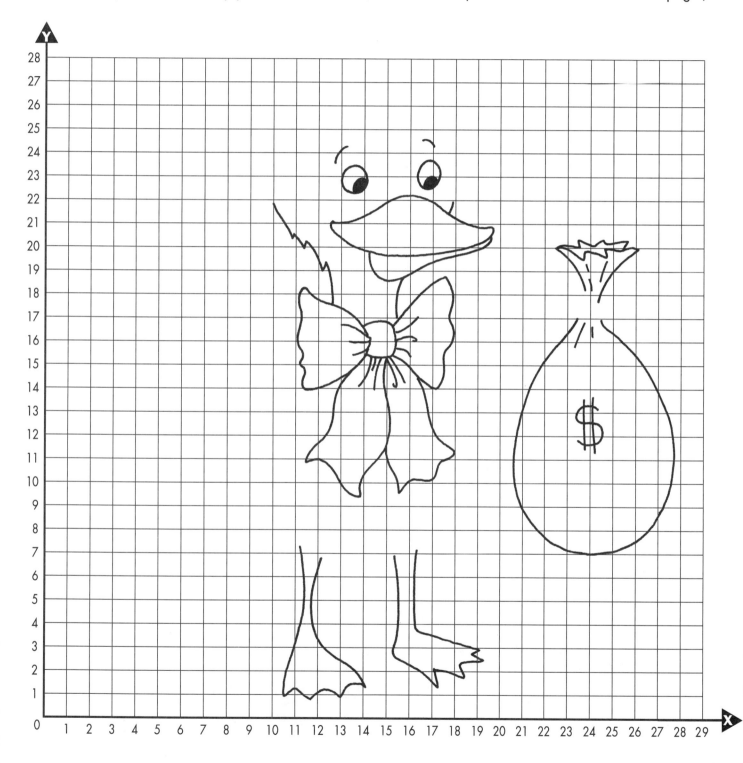

Answer: *All her friends have bills.*

Name_____

Banker

1. Look at number 1, right. The number in the first column is the X coordinate in an ordered pair.

2. On a separate sheet of paper, solve the problem in the second column. Rename the answer in lowest terms. The denominator in the answer is the Y coordinate.

3. Write the X and Y coordinates in the third column to make an ordered pair. The first one has been done for you.

4. Determine the ordered pairs for the rest of the chart.

5. Plot the ordered pairs on the graph on page 59 in the order they are given. Then use a straightedge to connect the points in the order you plotted them. When you come to the word "STOP," start a new line. Can you solve the riddle?

	X Coordinate	Y Coordinate	Ordered Pair
1.	10	$\frac{15}{2} \div 11 = \frac{15}{22}$	(10, 22)
2.	10	$\frac{1}{6} \div 4 =$	
3.	11	$\frac{7}{13} \div 2 =$	
4.	13	$\frac{2}{3} \div 9 =$	
5.	15	$\frac{4}{9} \div 3 =$	
6.	17	$\frac{11}{13} \div 2 =$	
7.	18	$\frac{15}{1} \div 23 =$	
8.	18	$\frac{9}{1} \div 22 =$	STOP
9.	18	$\frac{5}{6} \div 3 =$	
10.	20	$\frac{15}{1} \div 19 =$	
11.	23	$\frac{8}{1} \div 19 =$	
12.	25	$\frac{11}{17} \div 1 =$	
13.	21	$\frac{13}{1} \div 17 =$	
14.	19	$\frac{2}{5} \div 3 =$	
15.	20	$\frac{2}{1} \div 13 =$	
16.	20	$\frac{6}{10} \div 2 =$	
17.	16	$\frac{20}{5} \div 7 =$	
18.	12	$\frac{6}{1} \div 7 =$	
19.	8	$\frac{5}{9} \div 5 =$	
20.	6	$\frac{10}{4} \div 6 =$	
21.	6	$\frac{12}{1} \div 13 =$	
22.	7	$\frac{3}{7} \div 2 =$	
23.	9	$\frac{9}{13} \div 3 =$	
24.	10	$\frac{15}{6} \div 7 =$	
25.	9	$\frac{14}{3} \div 5 =$	
26.	5	$\frac{11}{5} \div 3 =$	
27.	8	$\frac{14}{1} \div 17 =$	
28.	10	$\frac{8}{17} \div 2 =$	
29.	11	$\frac{1}{4} \div 4 =$	

Great Graph Art: Decimals and Fractions Scholastic Professional Books

Create a Design: Part 1

1 Draw a simple picture on the graph that uses nine or ten points. (You can use more points after you become more experienced at creating graph designs.)

2 Beside each point on the graph, write the name of the ordered pair in parentheses.

3 Record the ordered pairs on page 62.

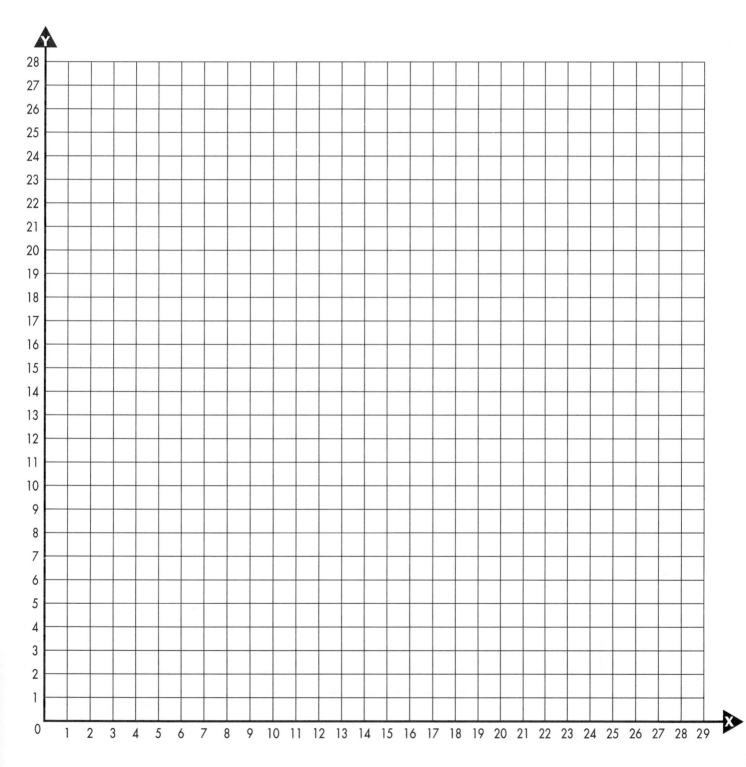

Create a Design: Part 2

1 First complete the activity on page 61.

2 On the lines below, write the ordered pairs in the order that the points should be connected.

3 When you want to end a line, write "STOP."

1.	
2.	
3.	
4.	
5.	
6.	
7.	
8.	
9.	
10.	
11.	
12.	
13.	
14.	
15.	
16.	
17.	
18.	

Answers

Page 5: **Baseball and Birthdays**

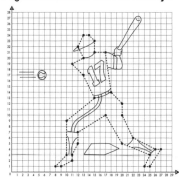

Page 7: **The Breakfast of Scarecrows**

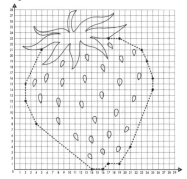

Page 9: **High Flier**

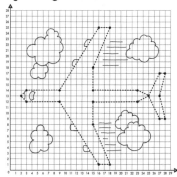

Page 11: **Speedy Traveler**

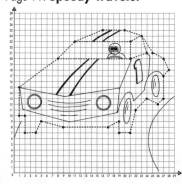

Page 13: **Heart Attack**

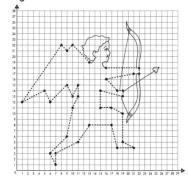

Page 15: **Homework Helper**

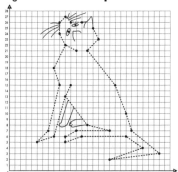

Page 17: **Mouse Trap**

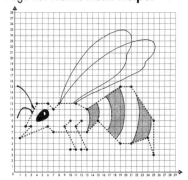

Page 19: **Rodeo**

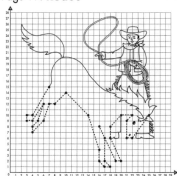

Page 21: **Glowing Grin**

Page 23: **New Job**

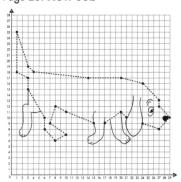

Page 25: **Take Off!**

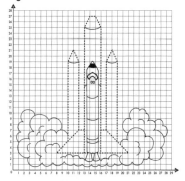

Page 27: **Practice Makes Perfect**

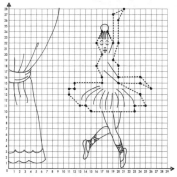

Page 29: **Solar System**

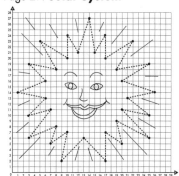

Page 31: **Flower Shop**

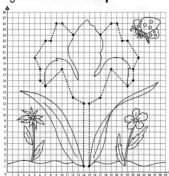

Page 33: **Vacation**

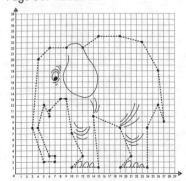

Page 35: **Ship's Friend**

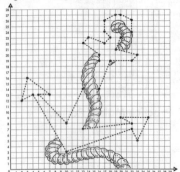

Page 37: **Ice Cream Parlor**

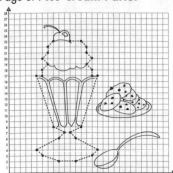

Page 39: **What Am I?**

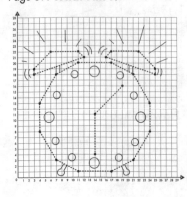

Page 41: **Lost Job**

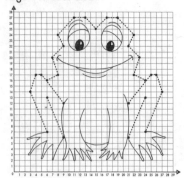

Page 43: **Boating**

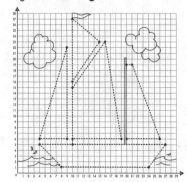

Page 45: **World Wide Web**

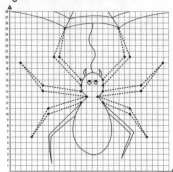

Page 47: **Bad Habits**

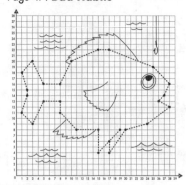

Page 49: **Shoemaker**

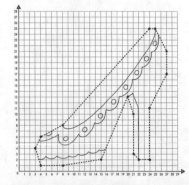

Page 51: **Zoo Friends**

Page 53: **Giant Fish**

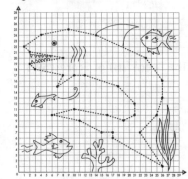

Page 55: **Mystery Bear**

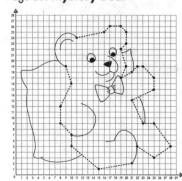

Page 57: **Pierre the Great**

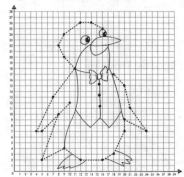

Page 59: **Banker**

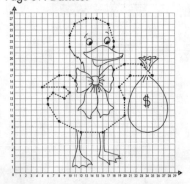